Proverbs for Living a Fulfilling Life:
WHAT I WISH SOMEONE HAD TOLD ME EARLIER

By

Rick Upchurch

PROVERBS FOR LIVING A FULFILLING LIFE: WHAT I WISH SOMEONE HAD TOLD ME EARLIER

Copyright © 2019 by Rick Upchurch: rlupchurch@gmail.com

Published by Tools to Lead Publishing

Printed in the United States of America

All rights reserved. No part of this publication may be reproduced, stored in a retrieval system or transmitted in any form or by any means – for example, electronic, photocopy, recording – without prior written permission of the author. The only exception is brief quotations for research purposes.

ISBN: 978-0-9833239-6-9

Contents

Introduction 1

Things are rarely as they seem to be 6

Simple solutions are better than complex ones 7

Suspect others may be smarter than you are 8

Honesty is the best policy 9

Content 10

Saying No 11

Listen more than you talk 14

The Sweetest Sound 15

Don't react defensively when confronted . 16

Do unto others as you would have them to do unto you 17

Inertia 18

Exceed Expectations 19

Everybody needs a mentor 22

Stress will always find a way to express itself in your life 23

Management by Walking Around (MBWA) 24

Teachable Spirit 25

Take a Time Out 26

Garbage in / Garbage out 27

DO IT!..30

Righteousness: the New Business Ethic....31

Provocation and Response 32

Watch the eyes...33

Handling the Flood..................................34

What are you waiting for?........................35

Email Communication 38

Handshake...39

Dress appropriately 40

Ponder BEFORE Responding...................41

To Policy, or not to Policy?.......................42

General Practical Proverbs 43

Tasks Which Define Success (TWDS) 46

Pay Attention to Personal Hygiene 47

Good grammar matters............................48

Attitudes are contagious 49

That's Just Who I Am...............................50

Taking and Giving Offense 51

Blood is Thicker than Water 54
Motivation 55
Smile 56
"Whose Fault is it?" 57
All of life can be reduced to relationships 58
Everyone has the same number of hours in a day 59
Leaders are learners 62
When to (or NOT to) Bleed 63
Defensive 64
Everything rises and falls on Leadership .. 65
Leaders make decisions 66
Multitasking = Mediocrity 67
Leaders take the initiative 70
Personal Reflection 71
Reputation 72
Add Value to Everything! 73
Intentional Influence 74
Social Media 75
Confrontation & Tears 79
"I'm Doing My Best" 80

Administrative Resolve 81

Expressed Appreciation 82

Put Your Oxygen Mask On 83

Be Present in the Moment 86

Persevere --Do not quit. 87

Public Speaking 88

Think Before You Criticize 89

Great Followers Make the Best Leaders 91

Leading Change 94

Scorpion and the Frog 95

Social Media 96

Language of RESPECT 97

Be Considerate of Others 98

Right 99

Gossip 102

Self-Sabotage 103

Taking Care of Business 104

Time Management 105

Complacency 106

Wisdom 107

Beware Precedent 110

You're Gonna Serve Somebody 111
Juggling 112
Compartmentalize 113
Urgency 114
Adversity 115
Sustainability 118
Technology 119
Grace, Mercy & Accountability 120
Are you Shouting? 121
The Greatest is Love 122
Take Care of Business 123
Self-Pity 126
Default Mode 127
The Brutal Truth 128
Eye Contact 129
Pick up the PHONE!!!! 130
Respect, Honor, & Love 131
Triangles 134
Politics 135
Stay in your Box 136
Family can drive you Crazy! 137

Expediency, Exigency, & Ethics 138
Mission Statement................................... 139
How to Treat Each Other 142
Leadership types..................................... 143
Good vs. Great.. 144
Get in the right seat................................ 145
Find the Balance..................................... 146
The Control of the Tongue 147
Economic Awareness 150
Making conversation 151
Generosity 152
Posture.. 153
Hire People Smarter Than You............... 154
Apologize 155
Pride Goes Before a Fall 158
WIIFM 159
Blind Spots – Johari Window 160
A Little Paranoia is Healthy 161
Before You Respond 162
In the Moment 163
Bad Company Corrupts 166

Don't Sell Yourself Short 167

Does Your Stuff Own You? 168

Credit and YOU 169

Fight of the two wolves........................... 170

Taking the Easy Road 171

You are a Steward.................................. 174

Worldview? 175

Going Somewhere? 176

Where Does the Bible Fit? 177

Email Terrorist....................................... 178

Execution: Key to Productivity............... 179

Conclusion... 183

Your Proverbs

_____	12
_____	20
_____	28
_____	36
_____	44
_____	40
_____	52
_____	60
_____	68
_____	76
_____	84
_____	92
_____	100
_____	108
_____	116

	124
	132
	140
	148
	156
	164
	172
	180

Introduction

Most of the proverbs contained in this book address the ability of an individual to be able to move forward in their career, achieve their potential and find a fulfilling life. Foundational to these proverbs, and explicitly stated in many of them, is the belief that a relationship with Jesus Christ as personal Lord and Savior makes a fulfilled life more likely. These proverbs are short, easy to read and, hopefully, will make you think. I have left blank pages throughout for you to record your own proverbs. There is also usually enough space on each page for you to insert your own thoughts or comments. If you do both, add comments to the printed proverbs and your own proverbs, this short book will become a friend you refer back to often, and one which will continue to benefit you through your entire career.

Because these proverbs are condensed to one page of material, they cannot describe all the nuances related to that topic. Whenever you find a topic with which you especially resonate, mark that topic for future study.

Please test the proverbs included in this book to see if they can bear the weight of real life application. I think you will find that they do.

Finally, here in the introduction let me clearly state that any positive information or impact I have or have ever made can be directly connected to the work of Jesus Christ in my life. In Him, I have my source and my life. Through Him I have attempted to be a light in the darkness, showing His love and living a life of faith, albeit imperfectly.

The Proverbs begins with a short summary of the Principles of Life, which is expanded upon in another of my books by the same title.

The proverbs contained in this book are directed at you improving you, bit by bit, in ways that will build personal confidence and transform your ability to interact with others. Think of these proverbs in terms of "what I wish I had been told about life when I was young", and you get the sense of what this book is trying to accomplish.

Principles of Life

I have made an effort to teach my children, and have passed on to hundreds of others, the importance of having life principles. By setting up life principles you will be more likely to succeed in whatever you undertake and enjoy your life more along the way. Specifically, I have five principles that could be called my core principles. Each of these principles are touched upon in at least one of the proverbs contained in this book. Most of these proverbs could be categorized using these principles. Whether or not you adopt the principles below as your own or develop others, I urge you to make this a priority in your life; you will not regret it!

The Principles of life are based upon the greatest commandment: "Love the Lord your God with all your heart, and all your soul, and all your strength and with all your mind; and, Love your neighbor as yourself." Luke 10:27 Probably, if we could figure out how to do this, then everything else in our life would naturally fall into place. Unfortunately, this is much more difficult that it appears. So the principles below are the boundaries I use for achieving that goal. They are infinitely expandable and you will see them throughout the proverbs in the remainder of this book.

Principles of Life
1. All of life can be reduced to relationships.
2. Everything rises and falls on leadership
3. Excellence in all things (do your best)
4. It is not what happens to you that counts but what you do about it (resilience)
5. Don't quit (perseverance)

Proverbs for Living a Fulfilling Life

Things are rarely as they seem to be

More often than not, our immediate impression of a situation or problem changes, sometimes 180 degrees, once we get more information. You probably have been the victim of this kind of snap judgement. The best advice is to avoid knee-jerk reactions and snap decisions until you have a better understanding of the situation. When you make a knee-jerk reaction or decision (emergencies excepted), it will almost always have some negative ramifications. Take a few moments to breathe; if necessary disengage or dampen your emotions so you can think. Ask some questions. Try to think about the situation from different perspectives, e.g. the way other individuals or groups would think about it. Particularly consider the motives of the key players, as this is often a key to finding a workable solution. What appears on the surface to be the problem is not necessarily the *real* problem; solving it may be like putting a Band-Aid on a broken arm, i.e. not very effective long-term. Taking even a few additional moments and gathering your thoughts, and any supplemental information, will make your decision better.

Simple solutions are better than complex ones

Simple solutions are typically better than complex solutions. The reason for this lies in two areas, first, the availability of resources needed to solve the problem, which includes time, material resources, and money is easier to resource if you keep things simple. Also included here but often overlooked is the availability of sufficient staff *with the appropriate skills to make the solution work*. Complex solutions often require expertise not readily available. Second, the execution of the solution, i.e., the ability and authority to follow-through to completion will be more likely to succeed if you keep it simple. The more people required and/or the more resources required, the more difficult the execution will be. The more time required to complete the plan, the greater the likelihood the plan will fail. Simple is usually better. So, because of limited resources, and the necessity of working with fallible people, who often have a different agenda, choose the solution that is the most simple to implement. It will also be the one most likely to endure.

Suspect others may be smarter than you are

You should always assume the person to whom you are speaking with is smarter than you are, or has access to more resources, information, or both. This is a good rule of thumb for every interaction and it guarantees you will not start the conversation by underestimating or demeaning others. Underestimating others, or thinking they are inferior in some way, is a common error made by pompous and arrogant leaders. Even if you know that on this point at least you do have superior knowledge, by not assuming you know it ALL, you might learn something that you did not know that will help you make better decisions. You are more likely to actually hear what is said and take it seriously when you assume that you are speaking with someone with superior wisdom. Regardless of how smart YOU are, or how much experience you have, there is always the possibility that you could learn something new. It is pompous and arrogant to assume you do not need the input of others. So, not only assume others may be smarter, be open minded enough to listen to what they have to say.

Honesty is the best policy

In fact, honesty is the ONLY policy! According to Kouzes and Posner in the *Leadership Challenge*, honesty is the most identified trait of leaders that others want to follow. It may not be the trait which gets you promoted, but it is definitely the trait that if not practiced will get you fired, or lead to divorce, or see you alone with no friends. Honesty takes courage. It can be difficult to be honest when a "little" lie will get you out of trouble. Being honest when faced with the easy option to lie is the mark of true character. Honesty really is the best (and only) policy. Being honest is a foundational character trait. It means telling the truth regardless of the consequences; even if the truth is that you failed. Being honest means you own up to failure when it happens, and take the consequences. If you made a mistake or dropped the ball on a project, admit it, apologize, take the consequences as the cost of learning and move on. Covering up mistakes or blaming others erodes your leadership and your soul. Honesty is the best policy. A person who lacks honesty cannot be trusted. This is not a reputation you want.

Content

Paul, the Apostle, states, "I have learned to be content whatever the circumstances. I know what it is to be in need, and I know what it is to have plenty. I have learned the secret of being content in any situation…" (Phil. 4:11-12) The secret to being content to which he is referring is a complete faith in Jesus Christ; absolute trust that God is at work for the best. Not much of a secret, but definitely a significant commitment. We each exist in a reality that probably is not how we imagined or hoped it would be. No doubt, there are some aspects of your life that could even be described as tragic. You are not alone, however, our unpleasant realities are *only* unpleasant because we refuse to accept them as pieces in a greater puzzle. We are prevented from accepting and moving forward by denial; "I don't want to believe this is happening, so I'll pretend it isn't happening and hope it goes away." Alternatively, avoidance: "I don't like what is happening and don't want to be part of it." Neither denial nor avoidance will change our reality, but faith in God can change our perspective and even give our reality meaning.

Saying No

In 2014, CVS Pharmacy said NO to carrying tobacco products. Their announcement included this sentence: "The sale of tobacco products is inconsistent with our purpose – helping people on their path to better health." Their decision was definitely controversial and cost the company $2 billion a year in direct sales. Having the guts to say NO to anything can be difficult; saying no to $2 billion dollars requires laser-like focus on your core principles. Saying NO, and meaning it, comes more easily to some than others, but it can be easier for anyone *if* they know they core values and place them before any other consideration. What makes your core values *CORE*, is that you believe they express who you are and who you were meant to be. It is a matter of belief and conviction. The other side of that coin is that your core values can also guide you in saying YES as well. If you are one of those who find it difficult to say NO, review your own core values, make sure you write them down, and then use them to give you the strength you need to say NO, as well as the courage to say YES when the situation demands it. Doing this will give you an inner peace even when things are in chaos.

(Your Proverb)

Listen more than you talk

Listening more than talking is hard for anyone, but especially hard for some. Most of us seem to like the sound of our own voice. I want to encourage you to STOP talking and listen, not merely listen, but to listen *intensely*, *fiercely* listen. Listen not just to the words being said but also to the emotions behind them. Pay attention to the choice of the words used. Ask questions to clarify what you think you heard; DO NOT assume anything. Really listen until you have heard, and then listen some more. If you can repeat the information back in different words with the same emotional content, you *might* have heard what was said. Only then will you be able to respond effectively. One main problem in listening is our own ego. We are so convinced it is all about "me," that truly listening to anyone else is difficult. Instead of listening, we are trying to figure out what we are going to say when the other person finally quits talking. Who would you would label as a good listener? What do they do that makes you feel you are being heard? What does it feel like to be truly heard? You have the power to do that for others.

The Sweetest Sound

Dale Carnegie said that the sweetest sound to a person is the sound of their own name. I know when someone remembers my name I am impressed that they have taken the time and energy to do so; it adds to my impression of their credibility. One thing is sure: people who discipline themselves to learn and use the names of others in conversation give themselves an edge in dealing with people. The ability to remember names is often discounted as not that important, but it is probably one of the most important skills a leader can develop. It is particularly significant for those who understand the importance of relationships. The best way to remember a name is to listen carefully when you hear the name, repeat it back, associate it with something about the person, and use it as often as possible in talking to that person. Do not worry if you forget a name. Simply apologize for not remembering and ask them again for their name. People understand about forgetting and respect that you are making an effort to remember their name at all. Do not make excuses about why you cannot do this--just do it!

Don't react defensively when confronted

Eventually someone will confront you about some action you have taken or something you have said. In your mind this may or may not seem be to fair. Let me clarify something: *your perception at this point is meaningless*. Until you understand the perspective of the one confronting you, it will be impossible to move to a resolution. Do not give a list of reasons (excuses) for whatever you are being confronted. Do not blame ANYONE else, even if there is just cause to do so. Do not raise your voice, begin to cry, hit something, or walk off. Instead, take a deep breath, ask questions for clarification and then say "Thank you for being willing to share this with me. I will definitely consider what you've said." Then do just that: consider, what was said and learn from the experience. You are not perfect, no one is, and there is always room for improvement. If you always respond, defensively pretty soon no one will go to the trouble of giving you this necessary input. When that happens you are going to hit a glass ceiling in your career and relationships.

Do unto others as you would have them to do unto you

This is called the Golden Rule. Those who practice the Golden Rule in every part of their life are worth their weight in Gold! They recognize the significance of relationships and the value of personal integrity. Let us go one-step farther; do unto others, as you would like others to do unto your mother, daughter, or other loved one. When we treat others as we would like to be treated, or the way we would like our loved ones treated, not only do they love it, but also there is an inner affirmation that we have done the right thing. Remember this: all of life can be reduced to relationships. By practicing the Golden Rule you make it clear that you understand the value of each person and that they are as worthy as you are of respect and decency. We are all created in the image of God, and we are all bound together in intricate dependencies of mutual need. By treating others, as you would like to be treated you are reaching the higher levels of personhood and evidencing the presence of God in the world.

Inertia

Newton's first law of motion, also called the law of inertia, is often stated as "An object at rest tends to stay at rest, and an object in motion tends to stay in motion and in the same direction unless acted upon by an outside force." Newton's law was directed at physical objects, however, there is a lesson here which applies to processes and people as well. For instance, any process may eventually become so routine and formalized that it turns into bureaucratic dogma. When this happens, changing the process can be difficult, or nearly impossible. The law of inertia also applies to people, perhaps even more so. Henry Ford is quoted as saying, "Whether you think you can, or you think you can't – you're right." The meaning here is that we are constantly affected by the inertia of our minds. If we believe we are not capable of accomplishing much, the inertia of that belief will guarantee its accuracy. The only hope we have is the impact of an outside force. Many times that outside force is a crisis of some kind, e.g. a death, a birth, health issues, loss of a job, etc. Buy it can also include wise counsel and good friendships.

Exceed Expectations

It is a little known fact that everyone forms subconscious expectations regarding EVERYTHING and EVERYONE! This might not be so bad, except that our expectations are rarely accurate, and usually predispose us to place people and everything else into boxes. We form an expectation of a coworker or employee that they are consistently late, make the same kind of errors over and over again, or lack competence in certain areas, etc. Before you know it, our expectations become the label for that person, event, or thing in our mind. When that happens, it is nearly impossible to see past the label into new possibilities. You may be surprised to know that you are the victim of the same kind of judgement in the minds of your coworkers, friends, and supervisors. You are gauged and labeled. The best way to overcome this judgement is to strive to exceed the expectations of the responsibilities given to you. If the expectation is to be on time, then be early. If the expectation is to attend a meeting, attend AND be engaged. You can set the bar higher, which will always come back to bless you as your reputation for going above and beyond becomes known.

(Your Proverb)

Everybody needs a mentor

Really, everybody needs multiple mentors across their entire life. So make it your goal to get as many mentors as possible, in various areas of your life: professional, faith, parenting, recreational, etc. I have had a few that deeply influenced my life. All of my mentors taught me important lessons about what to do and how to live. From some I learned lessons about what *not* to do and practices to avoid. Not all my mentors are, or were, living people. Some, like Jesus, lived thousands of years ago but their impact has come through their recorded words. I do not think I was very successful at finding or connecting with as many living mentors as I could have. Mostly my mentors affected my life through what they had written and what had been written about them. There are many good books that can serve as substitute mentors if you are willing to "listen" and learn. Probably the best place to start is a regular cycle of reading through the New Testament at least every year. If you think you do not need a mentor or cannot benefit from the wisdom of others, you are wrong, ignorant, and quite possibly stupid.

Stress will always find a way to express itself in your life

Stress might show up in weight gain, weight loss, nail biting, teeth grinding, illness, headache, grouchy attitude, etc. This is true no matter the type of stress (good or bad, short-term or long-term) or the source of stress (work, kids, money, spouse, parents, car, etc.). It will usually evidence itself the same way in your life. For example, in overeating or nail biting, so learn your stress signs. There are as many ways to reduce stress as there things which cause stress: exercise, watching a movie, talking to a friend, taking a nap, taking a bath, listening to music, drinking some tea, etc. There is also many unhealthy ways to reduce stress, which will eventually cause you even more stress: over-eating, under-eating, alcohol consumption, non-prescribed medications, extramarital sex, etc. Once you know how you react to stress, you have a better chance of noticing your reaction and taking the appropriate measures to reduce the stress. One thing is for sure – you can never fully eliminate it, but with some practice, you can manage it so it does not derail your life.

Management by Walking Around (MBWA)

MBWA is a tried and true business practice, which is part of every good leader's regular activities. It means, do not sit at our desk all day managing through reports alone. You may not be a manager, yet, however, you should be aware that you could not truly lead or manage people without being involved, after all, "all of life can be reduced to relationships." Reports and data analysis are important- but it is people who get the job done and relationships, which provide energy, not to mention accountability. Get up and walk around, get to know people and the work of your business - it will make a difference. Talk with those at every level of your organization and build relationships. Listen to what they have to say and ask their opinions about how to improve their work or the organization in general. Show a genuinely caring spirit. Make follow-up notes in your contact manager of important facts and NEVER fail to give credit if you take an idea and put it into practice. MBWA builds credibility like few other things.

Teachable Spirit

A former mentor, Dr. John Conley, once told me that you could recognize true leaders by how they receive correction and guidance: People with a teachable spirit are able to learn from their mistakes and grow to become better. People without a teachable spirit are always defending themselves, and blaming circumstances or others for their failures. If you do not have a teachable spirit, you will constantly wonder why you are being picked on, persecuted… or avoided. In fact, if you regularly feel picked on or persecuted by your superior, it could be a sign that you do NOT have a teachable spirit. Henry Cloud calls these people fools. Fools may be very intelligent, but if they cannot or will not learn, cannot or will not accept responsibility and grow from correction, then they are indeed fools. A teachable spirit only comes when we are willing to let go of our egos and be open to the fact that we still have some things to learn. Those with a teachable spirit are also called humble. If you can humble yourself to listen to correction and accept your need to improve there may be hope for you.

Take a Time Out

When you are in the middle of a stressful situation that is on the verge of overwhelming your ability to respond appropriately, STOP. It is far better for you to take a short time out than to say, or do, something that you will later regret. There is no harm or blame in knowing yourself well enough to know when it is the best choice to hit the pause button. This can be as simple as saying, "Excuse me for just a minute (while I make a quick call, use the restroom, think about what you have just said, etc.)," and then step out of the situation for as long as necessary to find your personal balance. While this is the best option, sometimes you literally cannot separate yourself physically from the situation. If that is the case, then another tactic is to slow things down by taking a couple of deep breaths, exhaling slowly. This provides extra oxygen to your brain and enables you to think a little more clearly. Another tactic is to create a distraction by asking a question not specifically related to the situation. Or, try a reflecting question like "Let me make sure I understand what you are saying" and repeating it back. All of these can help you stay in control of you.

Garbage in / Garbage out

Garbage in/Garbage out is an older phrase introduced in the early days of computer programming. It meant that if your programming was bad, garbage in, then your output would also be bad, garbage out. This phrase has also been applied to people, as well. Health-wise the phrase "you are what you eat" reflects the same awareness that our diet affects our overall health and physical well-being. The concept also finds a parallel in how we think. Let me give you an example. I was reading a thrilling piece of fiction and found my heart speed increasing and my nerves responding like I had been chewing on coffee beans. What was coming in the story was generating a physical and emotional response. Controversies over the impact of video games on those who play them fall into this category. The bottom line in is that we are affected by what we see, read, and hear; it generates a response that is not merely physical but also emotional, affecting our attitudes and behaviors. The wise person will consider this and limit their exposure to the kind of things that detracts from their ability to live a righteous life that would be pleasing to God and our own self-worth.

(Your Proverb)

DO IT!

If your boss asks you to do something, unless it is unethical or immoral, DO IT! Do whatever is asked with excellence and ahead of schedule. You may not understand why you were asked to do that specific task, or you may feel that the task is beneath you. Either way, that is not your call. Your call is to be an exemplary employee, or find a different job. Do not turn a molehill into a mountain. Here is a great secret: Bosses do not always make sense, you will not either when you are the Boss! The important thing is that you do what is asked of you to the best of your ability, with a positive attitude, preferably under budget and ahead of schedule. (Just a suggestion, always, always deliver ahead of schedule.) Use Joseph from the Bible as your inspiration and consider his performance while a slave in Egypt. When put into difficult circumstances, he responded in every case by giving his best. He didn't question or complain. He did earn a reputation for excellence. If you do not understand what you are supposed to do, ask for clarification. If you are not capable of performing what is asked of you, let your boss know. Otherwise, just DO IT, and do it to the best of your ability.

Righteousness: the New Business Ethic

Ethical practice seems to imply righteousness. I know that is not the *definition* of ethical behavior, but it is what most of us would *understand* when someone is said to be ethical, that is, that they behave rightly. When ethical practice actually does equate with righteousness, then things go well, the business prospers and God is honored. However, when your personal or business ethic deviates from righteousness, trouble is not far behind. Most people know the difference between right and wrong but too often that does not stop some from ignoring what they know in their heart. In Mark 7:9-13 the Pharisees were twisting their ethics so that instead of pursuing what was right, they were able to rationalize unrighteous behavior. Sadly, it is not uncommon for people to convince themselves they are justified to modify their perception of what is right. *A true ethic will always promote righteousness and love* - beware of the pseudo-ethic that seems rational, but only covers up selfishness and greed. Just focus on righteousness as defined in the Bible and you should be fine.

Provocation and Response

Imagine your boss comes to you irate over something you have done, or not done. From your perspective, the issue did not seem to be significant enough to warrant your boss' tone of voice, or choice of words. Which takes me to my point: *If the response seems out of proportion to the provocation, then you should strongly suspect there are other factors contributing to the response and not take it personally.* Those factors can range from health to childhood baggage, from family or work stress to any of a myriad of other things. **The important thing is not to respond in kind**, i.e. just because someone is yelling at you does *not* mean you have to yell back. Responding in kind can escalate a situation out of proportion to its significance and damage relationships beyond repair. When the response is greater than the provocation, keep in mind that we are all people and it is likely some other issue or issues which are coming into play. Forgive, as you have been forgiven (by Christ) and move forward. Alternatively, to put it another way: Do not make a mountain out of a molehill.

Watch the eyes

I am not talking about eye contact, although that is important. What I am talking about is being aware of who has influence and where the lines of power within a meeting/organization fall. There is no way to escape politics; wherever two or more people are gathered together, politics is also present. Leadership is about influence and while title figures into the equation, it is by no means the whole story. To figure out who has the most influence watch the eyes. When you are in a meeting, watch the eyes of all those in the meeting, especially those asking questions, to see who get the most attention. That person, regardless of title, is the primary influencer, i.e., the leader. If you thought you were the leader and you are not the one getting the attention then you can be assured that someone else has more influence that do you. If you want to increase your influence, you need to work hard at establishing strong working relationships with your team and establish credibility, the subject of another proverb. Learn to work together and eventually you may become the leader your title says you are.

Handling the Flood

Handling the flood of information that comes at you on any given day can be challenging, or even overwhelming. You receive an email or file attachment you want to keep, but then forget where you have saved it. You place an important document or object in a "safe" place only to forget where that is. It is not just you; it is all of us. It is not because we are getting old and forgetful, although that may be true, but more likely because there is simply more to remember and keep track of in our lives than ever before in history. This is not likely to change, so we need to accept this as the new norm. To cope with the flood we need to construct processes and patterns in our lives to deal with all this information. For example, set up folders in your email account and immediately move email into the correct folder or delete it. Organize your computer desktop into folders. One of the best solutions is to use a cloud service like Evernote or OneNote and save all your stuff with a variety of "tags" so you can search and find it later. The flood will sweep you away if you let it – so take charge!

What are you waiting for?

It has been said that if you put a frog into a large pot of water, and slowly bring it to a boil, the frog will make no effort to escape, eventually dying even though escape was readily available. Actual empirical evidence indicates this story is not true; but it makes a great leadership example about how easy it is for us humans to remain in our ruts, that is, our patterns of behavior, even when they are detrimental to our stated goals or health, and even when we could change our behavior and improve our situation. Take for instance the chronic smoker who refuses to change even though her habit drastically increases the likelihood of cancer. Or, the man who refuses to evacuate in the face of an approaching hurricane, or forest fire and dies because of that decision. As a rule, we are all more comfortable with just keeping things the way they are, even while complaining about our circumstances. Only the brave will face their reality and choose to act, to embrace new behaviors and thoughts that can lead to a better life. So, stay in the pot and boil, or take a chance and jump out into a new opportunity.

(Your Proverb)

Email Communication

When communicating by email to anyone (work, family, friends, colleagues, etc.), ALWAYS re-read the email at least once before you send it, preferably twice! If it is particularly important or going to a supervisor or a large group, read it over several times, at least one of which is aloud. When you read your email aloud you will get a better sense of the tone of voice and more easily catch grammatical errors. Tweak the wording until it actually communicates in the clearest possible, and least offensive, terms possible the message you mean to convey. It is surprising how many people think a terse email actually communicates their message. Usually, the terse, abrupt email raises more questions than it answers and can even create an unexpected level of anxiety. Think carefully about how various recipients will interpret your choice of words, and what "attitude" they may read into the way you put the words together. This process will take a little longer but will result in better responses, actions, relationships, etc., not to mention avoiding unexpected relationship difficulties.

Handshake

First impressions make a difference. One of the things that contribute to that first impression is the handshake. It may sound ridiculous, but when you shake hands with someone, who gives you a limp handshake, part of you immediately assumes that the individual may have low self-worth or lack self-confidence. Similarly, when you shake hands with someone who immediately tries to crush you hand, the automatic assumption is that they are overcompensating for some insecurity, or trying to intimidate you in some way. You would think that everyone already knows this, but when greeting with a handshake, make sure it is firm, with a clear grip: not too hard, not light. Do not try to crush their hand and do not be a dead fish. Be conscious of those who may have arthritis or other similar conditions. While shaking hands look the other person directly in the eyes. Hold eye contact for at least a full second if not two; be totally present in that moment. You will find this combination very effective in communicating your sincerity and a contribution to credibility.

Dress appropriately

Dress appropriately for whatever position you hold at the place you work. What is being worn at other companies is not a factor in what is appropriate for where you are currently working. They may be wearing jeans or suits at the company across the street, while at your place of employment everyone dresses the opposite. IT DOES NOT MATTER. This is one area where conformity to the approved style is important. You can vary within certain boundaries, but go too far and you will limit your ability to move up, at the very least, or even stay employed in the worst-case scenario. It may seem ridiculous to you, but failure to pay attention to this can undermine your credibility without you even knowing it. If you do not like the dress code--get a different job. The only exceptions to this of which I am aware is higher education faculty, or those who work in tech development, who can pretty much dress however they like. I would go so far as to say, "Dress appropriately for the position *to which you aspire* at that company." By doing this you position yourself as someone that others, particularly your supervisor(s) could see in that role.

Ponder BEFORE Responding

A knee jerk response to an offending statement has been the source of many a leader's downfall, particularly if that response is caustic or unfounded. Responding this way can label you as emotional and shows lack of good judgement. Being labeled as someone lacking good judgement can be a career killer. If you are responding to an offensive statement or challenging email: DO NOT, at least until you have some time to ponder what was said. Simply saying, "I need some time to consider what you've said," will give you the time to make a more considered response. Ponder the offending statement from several angles. Could it have a different meaning? What else could it mean? What could have prompted it? Is it like this person to make this kind of statement? Is the statement out of proportion to the subject? Consider all this **before** responding, and if possible sleep on it before you respond. When responding, choose your words to *focus on the issue, not attack the person*. You will avoid a lot of blunders and pain by following this plan.

To Policy, or not to Policy?

Sometimes a policy is *exactly* what you need. Policies can provide valuable guidelines for corporate behavior that helps keep everyone on the same page and moving the same direction. Of course, having a policy but not enforcing it can be worse than not having a policy at all. However, not all situations require or are best served by having a policy. There is a tendency, especially among new leaders, to try to *manage by policy.* Managing individual people by implementing complicated and detailed corporate policies, that is policies that affect everyone in the company, is counterproductive, and almost never works. If you can approach an individual directly about their conduct or behavior, and address it one-on-one, you are far better off than setting up a policy that can have a negative effect on morale for the majority, inhibiting creativity and innovation. Determine if the undesired behavior is widespread and negatively affecting production, morale, or the culture; if so, then a policy may be necessary. If not, then either ignore it, or address it with the one or two bad actors. This is the burden of true leadership.

General Practical Proverbs

Here are some statements you might want to refrain from saying or asking: NEVER say anything bad about your old boss, or previous significant other. NEVER ask a woman that you do not know for sure is pregnant when she is due, or how is the pregnancy going. NEVER call your coworkers, employees, or children stupid. NEVER use humor to disguise an insult directed at your supervisor, spouse, or anyone else. ALWAYS believe that any negative complaint you make regarding your boss or coworkers will be repeated. REMEMBER two people CAN keep a secret, if one of them is dead, otherwise, not so much. NEVER lie for expediency's sake – it will ALWAYS come back to bite you, in fact NEVER lie, period. ALWAYS try to put a positive spin on everything, even if you suspect the opposite is true. Positivity can be a powerful door opener for influence. BE CONSERVATIVE in your speech and respectful to everyone. REMEMBER using humor directed at ANYONE other than yourself will almost certainly offend someone, and sometimes even if it is self-directed. ALWAYS arrive a little early and leave a little late.

(Your Proverb)

Tasks Which Define Success (TWDS)

There are some tasks that will make the difference between success and failure: at home, work, and life in general. These are the Tasks Which Define Success. Do those tasks well, and success is assured. Fail to do those tasks, or do them poorly, and mediocrity or even failure are in your future. You may be very busy, but not very successful. This is true in EVERY situation and area of your life. Figuring out WHICH Tasks Define Success is probably the most important thing you will do in any endeavor. In a marriage there are many important things that make a marriage work, *but fidelity tops the list;* get that wrong and it can all crumble. The TWDS are not always so easy to figure out, especially in a new job or situation. You may have to talk candidly with your supervisor to get this information. For eternity, the number one TWDS is to accept Jesus as your personal savior. In every part of your life, take some time to analyze what you do and what your Boss expects, and then make sure to get the TWDS done first!

Pay Attention to Personal Hygiene

Personal hygiene refers to how you care for our body and includes such things as bathing, brushing your teeth, hair care, etc. Probably this topic is too basic to include here, but this is also one of the areas where no one may ever tell you why you are not being included, or why you have been passed over for promotion. Chronic bad breath is off-putting, as is dirty greasy hair, or obvious body odor. None of these things are difficult to address, but if neglected can definitely impact your relationships, particularly in a professional setting. If you have chronic bad breath, see a dentist as there is usually a reason. Take a shower. Wash your hair. Make yourself presentable. I think about the main character in the movie the Pursuit of Happiness, who even though with almost nothing understood the importance of this concept and made every effort to present himself in the best light possible, part of which was a focus on personal hygiene. Let's face it, if you smell bad, and look bad, no one may ever get past those barriers to discover the truly wonderful person you really are.

Good grammar matters

Using good grammar matters in your writing, and it matters in your speech. Poor grammar will have a limiting effect on your career, and do so in a way that you may never know why you are not progressing. Being able to communicate effectively requires you to understand and use good grammar in all forms of communication. If you are not sure if you are speaking or writing with appropriate grammar, find a good friend, someone you know from personal experience who does use good grammar, who will tell you the truth, and have him or her call you out when you use poor grammar in your speech. Same with your writing...have someone proofread what you write until you get this conquered. Listen to how those you admire write and speak and use that as a model for developing your grammar. One of the best ways to improve grammar is to read well-written fiction. As you read the dialogue of the characters put yourself in their position and try out the words and phrasing. Practice your new skills daily. An articulate person has a greater chance of being heard in any audience.

Attitudes are contagious

One of my supervisors once called me into his office and told me I had a negative attitude and needed to change that, and quickly. I was shocked! I thought I was so positive. This was a revelation for me, and I made some immediate changes in my attitude. Whether I agreed or not, I was being perceived as negative and it was affecting my influence . . . and my job! Attitudes are contagious, especially those of the leader. Negativity will sink the morale of everyone around you. It can creep up on you so subtly that you may not even realize it has become a prominent part of your perspective. Stop and check yourself daily, asking "am I displaying a negative attitude, a critical spirit, or constantly griping or whining about situations?" If you answer yes to any of the above, STOP IT! Confront negativity whenever it rears its ugly head, in yourself and in those who report to you. Some will only need to be reminded to be positive, while others may need to be dismissed for the good of the institution. Make sure you are not the one let go because of your negativity!

That's Just Who I Am

"I call 'em like I see 'em," "I'm direct, I say what I mean," "I don't pull my punches," "I'll tell it to you straight." Usually these kind of statements are followed by "that's just who I am." I think we can all appreciate being told the truth, but more often than not these kind of comments, and the vitriol that often accompanies them, amounts to nothing more than evidence of poor or nonexistent people skills (emotional intelligence). If you are wearing that phrase like a badge of honor, proud of your personal integrity, the only one you are fooling is yourself. This might come as a surprise, but it is possible to be genuine *and* truthful, and still not offend everyone you meet. It does mean, however, that you have to take responsibility for what you are saying and *how* you are saying things and begin to consider others. Paul, in the book of Philippians says, "…in humility consider others better than yourselves. Each of you should look not only to your own interests, but also to the interests of others." (Phil. 2:3b-4) YOU get to choose who you are, choose wisely or you will find your career stalled.

Taking and Giving Offense

When someone takes offense easily the aphorism is that "they wear their emotions on their sleeve," implying that their emotions are so near the surface that they are easily provoked. That provocation can come in any number of ways, for instance, a word, a facial expression, or even a touch can evoke a response seemingly out of proportion to the stimulus. People who wear their emotions on their sleeve are difficult to be around for any length of time because of the inevitability that something will eventually offend them and cause an emotional response. On the other hand, there are those who intentionally want to give offense and provoke emotional responses in others. Sometimes these individuals are oblivious to their impact. I can imagine a Mother's seemingly harmless comment to a Daughter-in-law regarding a diet. Other times the provocations are carefully planned for their disruptive effect. Both type of personalities are examples of an individual who has poor emotional intelligence. In both cases, the upward movement for that individual in their career will be limited. Emotional intelligence is a crucial, learnable, skill-set. I strongly encourage you to do some research in this area.

(Your Proverb)

Blood is Thicker than Water

Regardless of what anyone may say, blood is thicker than water. By that, I mean if you slight someone's family member, be prepared for battle. Whether it is true or not, the right or wrong of the case rarely matters, and rational thought does not often enter into the discussion. Even if you have been asked to give a fair evaluation of someone's family member, it will usually come out poorly if you have negative things to say. People will usually respond negatively when you critique any member of their family, even if it is deserved. Sometimes they will go so far as to blame and attack you. Therefore, the first thing you need to do when working with a group of people is find out who is related to whom. This will help you avoid putting your foot in your mouth and, at the very least, insulting someone or causing a major conflict that can negatively can affect the project, the institution, or other relationships. The second thing you need to do is deal with people directly in as clear a manner as possible and avoid speaking ill of anyone to others. Period!

Motivation

People are motivated extrinsically, by rewards of various kinds, or intrinsically by how achieving goals makes them feel. Intrinsic motivation includes feeling appreciated, feeling fulfilled, feeling as if you have contributed to another person's well-being, feeling like you are making a difference. Typically, intrinsic motivation is superior to extrinsic, as long as basic needs are being met. In other words, if basic needs are being met, most people respond better to intrinsic motivation. Trying to motivate someone with extrinsic rewards will never be as effective unless there is an accompanying intrinsic motivation that produces some positive feelings. For leaders this means to lead first by reinforcing intrinsic rewards. To do this you have to understand your direct reports and what is important to them, i.e. what are the values that they hold. Extrinsic rewards, for example: throwing money at a problem, will only go so far in achieving high performance, especially once an individual's basic needs are being met. Find the intrinsic motivation that fits, and then seek to deliver that and meeting your goals will follow.

Smile

Smiling at people will always, always, always have a better outcome than any other facial expression. Mother Teresa said: "I will never understand all the good that a simple smile can accomplish." Studies have shown that people who smile more had longer lasting marriages, better general well-being, lived longer, and were healthier. Smiling automatically generates smiles in return. People simply cannot help themselves; when they see a smile the natural response is to smile in return. When that happens you are better able to build a relationship. People perceive people who smile to be more confident and competent. In fact, employers tend to promote people who smile often! Honestly, there are a LOT of reasons to smile. Smiling is easy for some while others have to make a more conscious effort. If you are one of those to whom smiling does not come naturally, WORK ON IT until it becomes natural. This will benefit your career and make your life in general more enjoyable. A smile lights up the face and releases a kind of positive goodwill. Choose to smile.

"Whose Fault is it?"

The word: "Whose Fault is it?" should rarely, if ever, come out of your mouth. Very little good comes from laying blame. Blame is the response of poor leadership. It is indicative of someone who is more interested in self-validation and self-preservation, than success. Instead of blame, focus on **why** the problem happened, **what** led up to it, and **how** it can be avoided in the future; or fixed so that it does not happen again. Sometimes this means better accountability structures be put into place. Good leadership places accountability structures into place to move the project AND the person toward success. Other times it means shifting personnel so the right people are in the right spots. Not everyone is equally capable in every area and finding the right fit better insures personal job satisfaction and productivity. It might mean that resources need to be allocated differently in order to insure success. Think about this: if you are the leader, and you are saying "Whose fault is it?" the likely answer is that it is YOUR fault for not providing the right structures, training, and resources to insure success.

Principle of Life:
All of life can be reduced to relationships

This is a fundamental principle of life. Everything comes down to relationships. How we interact with others, and the quality of our relationships, is more indicative of potential success than how smart you are. Those who recognize this and work to maintain positive relationships are more likely to succeed, be healthier, happier, and have less stress in their lives. Even if that were not true (and it is!), our relationships with others reflects the quality of our relationship with God. God's call repeatedly expressed throughout the New Testament is to love others. Regardless of what you say or think, it is our responsibility and challenge to do all we can to have healthy relationships. Saying we love God and treating others with disrespect is contradictory and hypocritical. Some situations are out of our hands. Nevertheless, we can and should do all that is within our power to make sure we are treating others as if they too were made in the image of God.

Everyone has the same number of hours in a day

Here is an interesting exercise that I have found quite enlightening the times I have done it. Keep track of your day in a log accounting for every minute of your day in 15-minute blocks for a week. Log how much time you spent answering emails, on Facebook, talking with coworkers, making phone calls, eating, driving, watching TV, surfing the internet, etc. Log it all and BE HONEST, no one needs to see this but you so do not cheat to make yourself look better. What you find will surprise you; you will discover that you waste far more time than you thought. What you will also discover is that your are not TOO BUSY at all. Your "busy-ness" is nothing more than the lack of clear priorities and focus in your life. Remember, everyone has the same amount of time; to say "I'm too busy" is an insult to others who know you really are not busy, merely disorganized, or over-committed, or self-important (pompous). Honestly, whenever I hear someone use busy-ness as an excuse, it undermines my confidence in their competence.

(Your Proverb)

Leaders are learners

Leaders are learners, at least good leaders are. I mean this in the sense that Leaders never stop actively learning. Learning does not always come in the classroom, nor is it restricted to one specific subject or modality. Whether in the classroom, through reading professional journals, or books, listening to podcasts, or reading blogs, the best leaders are ALWAYS learning. I try to encourage everyone to be reading five books at the same time.

- Bible
- Devotional for spiritual insight
- Professional book related to your occupation (this might be a journal or a magazine)
- Book on Leadership
- Novel

Add to this list at least one podcast on a favorite professional subject. This diversity allows your brain to gain sufficient input to assist you in solving problems and making better decisions. Studies consistently show that those who have multiple inputs (i.e. information from different areas of life) are more successful in finding solutions and are more creative.

When to (or NOT to) Bleed

Think of a continuum with health at one end, then scratches, then minor cuts, then major cuts, then open wounds and finally, death at the other end. You can lose a little blood and still be fine. If you lose more blood, you will be weak. If you lose too much blood, you will be dead. This is a metaphor for dealing with political challenges at home and at work. By political challenges, I mean anything that involves making or negotiating a decision where you are invested in the solution. You will face these challenges often as a leader, and be called upon to make decisions that support or kill various initiatives. Knowing which ones are worth bleeding, or even dying for, is the mark of a mature and wise leader. Your values and mission should be major considerations. There are a LOT of good ideas, but not all of them can be, or should be, acted upon. If you cannot make this distinction you will likely "bleed" to death over inconsequential decisions. This leads to a stalled career and/or frequent job changes. You only have so much blood - spend it wisely.

Defensive

When challenged, if your first thoughts and words are to defend your actions, to offer reasons or excuses, or find someone to blame...you are being defensive. When you respond defensively, you effectively say that you are not qualified for leadership. If it happens often, you might as well be saying, "I'm not qualified for my position." Phrases like "I was just…"or "But you don't understand…" or "It's not my fault" are defensive phrases. To a supervisor you are saying you are more concerned about defending yourself than getting the job done, that you are more concerned about your pride than growing and leading. Responding defensively is a learned behavior, probably one you picked up as a child. It can be *unlearned* with practice. Step one: when challenged, LISTEN, do not begin building your defense. Step two: find a solution that is as much win/win as possible. Step three: determine what you can learn from the challenge for the future. Be a leader: take ownership and get the job done.

Principle of Life

Everything rises and falls on Leadership

EVERYTHING! It is easy to see this wherever you go. If something in your life is not going well, assume you have the ability to improve the situation. Ask yourself, "What can I do to lead myself, and or others to a different and better solution or practice." If good things are happening, it is because someone is exercising leadership (it might be you!). If mediocrity prevails, it is because someone is not leading very effectively (it might be you!). If bad things are happening, it is because someone is not leading (maybe you should start leading!). This applies to your work, to your family, to your home and especially to YOU! Do not be a victim who blames circumstances or others for their predicament. Instead, *choose* to lead. Look around you: everything rises and falls on leadership and you always have the choice to lead yourself even if you lead no one else. Do not accept the role of a victim to whom things happen, instead adopt the mindset of a leader who chooses to make a difference.

Leaders make decisions

In fact, that is one of the defining characteristics of a Leader: they make decisions. Leaders pull together information from a variety of sources and, based on their experience and education, they make a decision. Sometimes the decisions made are good ones and other times not so good. Typically, if your good decisions outweigh your not-so-good decisions you are going the right direction. While some leaders will get lost in "analysis paralysis," the best leaders understand that sometimes any decision is better than no decision. Good leaders know that some decisions will turn out to be wrong, but they also know that to not decide can be worse. The best leaders are willing to live with the consequences of their decisions without blaming others. Instead, they accept the failures as learning experiences and keep moving forward. No one grows, nor is anything ever accomplished without some failure along the way. So, gather as much information as you can, consult some experts if you have time, collaborate if at all possible for the best solutions, and then make a decision.

Multitasking = Mediocrity

Multitasking is doing two or more things at the same time. For example, watching television, reading a book or playing a video game, while listening to a lecture. A LOT of people swear that when they do this they are able to concentrate better, learn more, and are more productive. However, studies have shown that when you attempt to multitask, both activities suffer. That is, neither activity gets 100% of your attention. That may be okay in some circumstances, but it is definitely not okay in others. In fact trying to multitask when doing anything important is going to produce mediocre results. Mediocrity or "good enough" is the mantra of the multi-tasker. Multitasking = mediocrity. I know people like this. They can be assigned some responsibilities, but when I need something done with excellence, they are not my first choice. Just think, if you can do better than average when you are multitasking, what would happen if you were to devote your full attention to one task? Learn to balance your priorities and narrow your focus so you can give 100% to each activity as needed.

(Your Proverb)

Leaders take the initiative

If you had to reduce leadership to one word, what would it be? I have heard many different answers to that question, such as: influence, innovation, domination, manipulation, persuasion, problem-solver, etc. For me, I would have to say that leadership, in one word, is initiative. A leader is one whose nature compels them to take action toward, and responsibility for, a specified goal, and involves others in the achievement of that goal. There is a saying that "nature abhors a vacuum," meaning if there is an empty space, something will invariably find its way into that space. Leaders are like that. If there is an absence of leadership (the practice), someone (a person) will step forward to do what has to be done. That is a Leader. They may try to hold back, but in the end, a leader recognizes the responsibility to step up, especially if failure is likely to damage lives. Leaders take initiative to fill the gap and inspire others to join them. I think that might be part of what being created in God's image means. Not everyone will do this but you can tell leadership by those who do.

Personal Reflection

It has been said that Socrates is the author of the statement: "The unexamined life is not worth living." Whether or not that is true, it is certainly true that self-examination is a key component to developing wisdom and self-mastery. Foundational to self-examination is taking time for regular personal reflection. I recommend you build into your schedule some regular time when you can reflect about: who you are, who you are becoming, where your life is heading, the integrity of your relationships, and areas where you need to improve. Consider opportunities for personal growth and development. Ideally, this time for personal reflection should be about 1-3 hours once a month or so, alone, and in a place where you will not be disturbed. Shut off your phone and ask yourself hard questions about how you are doing in ethical and moral decisions; consider areas where you are not living up to your principles. Stay true to your values; if you see yourself drifting away from them, refocus. Journaling during these times of reflection can be very helpful.

Reputation

Benjamin Franklin said, "It takes many good deeds to build a good reputation, and only one bad one to lose it." Proverbs 22:1 states, "Choose a good reputation over great riches; being held in high esteem is better than silver or gold." Be aware of your personal reputation in the various areas of your life. This can be your family, your social circles, your work environment, etc. In each case, you have a reputation of being a certain type of person; in many cases it isn't the same reputation as you have of yourself. The more your reputation in these various parts of your life align, the more likely you are to be living by your stated values. The differences in reputation from one area to another highlight aspects of your character that need to be addressed. For example, if you have the reputation for being truthful and honest with one group and as a liar and a cheat with another, you have a problem. If you are not aware of how you are perceived by others then make getting this information a priority. A single lie, infidelity, or act of dishonesty can undo a lifetime of integrity. You may make excuses for yourself but no one else will. Choose wisely.

Add Value to Everything!

The uppermost thought in your mind as you approach any task, position, or responsibility should be "How can I add value." This applies to every part of your life. You should always be asking yourself, "How can you take my skills, experience, education, resources and add value to the lives of others." Adding value can be as easy as smiling when serving a customer. It can be extra attention in formatting a document, checking facts, presentation of a dish; the list goes on and on. Consistently adding value to everything you do makes you one of the most valuable individuals at your company and in your circle of friends. If adding value to everything you do is your motto and practice you will quickly become the star employee, primed for promotion. Commit to making life better in some way for others without any thought of return. Just do it! God has equipped you to be able to make a difference. He has given you unique abilities, skills, personality, and passions so that you can make a difference. Those on the receiving end of your efforts will be appreciative and you will be amazed at how it makes you feel. Try it – add value – start today.

Intentional Influence

John Maxwell defines Leadership with one word: Influence. What I know is that influence is the currency of achievement. The more influence you have, the greater your ability to achieve your goals, personal or professional. The reality is that unless you live on an uninhabited island, you are influencing others. It is impossible to be around another person without influencing them, and being influenced yourself. If you see people come to work late without repercussions, you are more likely to be lax in your own arrival time. If you are diligent about arriving on time, others see that and are influenced to do the same. Of course, your personal credibility is a factor in this scenario as well. The difference is that leaders understand the dynamic of influence and achievement and *consciously choose their actions and words with the intent to influence*. The more an individual remembers and practices intentional influence, the more likely it is that their goals are achieved. Think about how and whom you influence and what you can do or say to become more purposeful in that influence.

Social Media

If you do not have and use a social media outlet, such as Twitter, Instagram, or LinkedIn, etc., for personal and professional purposes you are missing a huge opportunity to share your experience and knowledge as well as draw upon the experience and knowledge of others. Having such an outlet and using it increases your credibility and benefits a larger audience. Benefiting the larger audience is a key part of social media. Your active participation, with relevant material, enriches the conversation and contributes to influence. I highly recommend you setup an account in Twitter and LinkedIn. In Twitter, follow thought leaders in your industry and use #hashtags when you post. On LinkedIn, post your resume and make connections with colleagues. In both cases, contribute posts relevant to your interests. Make sure these posts are worded in a way that promotes the image you are seeking to convey: that you are professional and competent. Also, make sure you understand that these posts will last as long as the internet does (forever??) so be careful what you write.

(Your Proverb)

Principle of Life

Excellence in All Things

The pendulum swing for all our actions ranges from no effort to a perfectionistic ideal that is impossible to achieve. The medium point of the pendulum swing is "good enough." Jim Collins wrote in his book "Good to Great" that "good is the enemy of great." His point is that when we achieve good, most think that is "good enough." I want to suggest there is a place beyond good, what I have called Excellent. Paul writes, "Whatever you do, work at with all your heart, as working for the Lord, not for human masters." Colossians 3:23 Make "Excellence in all things" your personal moto. Build a reputation of someone who does things right; as someone who puts their entire energy into the task; their whole heart. Consider every act from the perspective of how you would present your efforts to God for review. Your salvation does not depend on your works, but that does not mean that you should not put forth your best effort. Your reputation *will follow* you so always strive to excellence.

Confrontation & Tears

If you are a leader and you have not had this happen yet…..it will. Confronting people can be challenging and stressful. Sometimes the one confronted begins to cry. So, here is what I have learned from my personal experience and research on how to handle this situation.

1. Tears are a biological reaction and are difficult to consciously control. Do not judge the person as too sensitive or "emotional" if there are tears.
2. Ignore the tears or ask: "I see this conversation is upsetting you, would you like to re-schedule a time to discuss this issue?
3. Recognize the presence of tears can mean the individual is feeling insecure and threatened by the conversation.
4. Tears can mean, in rare instances, that there is an attempt to manipulate an outcome less severe than expected.
5. This is most important: Stay on script to accomplish your goal. That assumes that you approached the conversation with a goal in mind. Never approach a confrontation without a clear goal in mind.

"I'm Doing My Best"

Sometimes you will hear people say "I'm doing my best" or "I tried my hardest". Perhaps you have said these words yourself. Think about the last time you said those words – now be honest, was the effort you put forth really your BEST? What is sad is that more often than not those who say these words believe what they are saying. In actuality, the truth is different. In many if not most cases, what was attempted was not even close to being their "best." What does "trying your best/hardest" REALLY look like? The answer is a serious commitment of time, energy, and resources, usually accompanied by delayed personal gratification. "Best" means focused effort that pushes you; people who try their best go far beyond the normal to achieve a goal. Realistically few people try their best at anything. Mediocrity is, in reality, too often the norm. Blaming others, or circumstances, is more common, even among those claiming to be doing their "best". So, bottom line, do not say you are doing your best, or working your hardest, unless you are willing to put forth the effort to make it true.

Administrative Resolve

Administrative resolve is the willingness of leadership to make hard decisions and then *stick with them when the going gets tough.* Administrative Resolve is quite possibly the most important aspect of *effective* leadership. With Administrative Resolve, a strategy is defined and pursued to its end. Without Administrative Resolve, second-guessing and lack of focus results in mediocrity and failure. James 1:8 says, "A double minded man is unstable in all his ways." This applies to the man and to the organization. Perhaps you have experienced why this is so challenging yourself when you have made a tough decision to deny or restrict access to some things for your children, only to have to deal with their tears, tantrums, and pleading. It is hard to hold your ground in those cases. Even more so when you are the leader and a decision you have made is unpopular with key constituents. Yet it is only Administrative Resolve that will open the doors to change, and without change, any organization is ultimately doomed. Make a decision and stick with it.

Expressed Appreciation

Do you express appreciation to those you lead? How do you do it? How often do you do it? Here is an even more important question: Do others *feel* as if you appreciate them? Perception IS reality and if others do not feel appreciated, YOU are dropping the ball. The result of this failure in the end is lower employee engagement, lower productivity and higher employee turnover. We all want and need to be appreciated. For leaders, expressing appreciation is key to an effective and productive team. Gary Chapman & Paul White in The 5 Languages of Appreciation in the Workplace state, "When leaders actively pursue communicating appreciation to their team members, the whole work culture improves" (p.24). For that to happen the expressed appreciation needs to be 1) targeted to specific individuals, 2) be sincere, and 3) expressed in a way that matches the individual's personality (money is NOT always the best answer). "Gallup reports that almost 70 percent of the people in the United States say they receive no praise or recognition in the workplace." (p34) Confront the hard truth – are you part of the problem?

Put Your Oxygen Mask On

You know how on an airplane trip the flight attendant goes over the safety instructions before the flight begins? One of the instructions is to take care of your own oxygen mask before trying to help others. The point is that if you do not get oxygen yourself, you will be unable to help others, i.e. you cannot help anyone if you are passed out from lack of oxygen. If you apply this to other parts of your own life it could mean: eating right, sleeping enough, regularly exercising, etc. so that you will be healthy enough to be there for your family, your work, and your ministry. More importantly, I think it applies to keeping your relationship with God fresh and alive and as a top priority. You can become so busy *DOING*, and that even includes ministry, that you lose the connection necessary for *LIVING*. Focusing on relationships helps keep things in balance, particularly focusing on an active relationship with God. When we do that, we pour oxygen into our souls and are strengthened to face each challenge, and help others too. All of life can be reduced to relationships.

(Your Proverb)

Be Present in the Moment

Being present in the moment is one of the secrets of level five leaders. This skill is often ignored or discounted by those aspiring to leadership who are busy trying to be all things to all people. Great leaders know how to come fully into the moment and focus their attention, intelligence, and relational energies in working with people and issues. Although they may not do this in every circumstance, they know WHEN and HOW to do it in a way that makes people feel heard, and valued. Our society works against the ability to be fully in the moment. Pressures come from every side, all of which all seem to be urgent, requiring immediate attention. The result is a society where couples sit at dinner focused on their cell phones instead of talking to each other, or where executives sit in meetings texting on their phones instead of participating in the discussion. While there are many benefits from technology, one of the drawbacks is that it can prevent your brain from being present in the moment. Put your phone down and develop the skill to be FULLY present and unleash the power within you.

Principle of Life
Persevere --Do not quit.

No one wants to be labeled a "quitter," but there are times when EVERYONE has felt the pull to quit. It could be a job, a friendship, a project, an educational program, even a marriage. If you are human, you have fell the temptation to quit. Sometimes quitting is the right answer, *but most of the time real victory and growth take place when you are willing to persevere*, to stick with it, in spite of the temptation to quit. The saying "winners never quit and quitters never win" is truer that we would like to admit. The grass is NOT greener on the other side of the fence. The same problems you are experiencing now will follow you wherever you go, perhaps in a different form, but no less challenging. Angela Duckworth has completed a major study on what she calls GRIT. Look up her TED talk. Grit combines passion with perseverance. Her results show that people with GRIT are more successful AND more fulfilled. The 80s band Wilson Phillips advises, "Holh On" for one more day. Sometimes that is all it takes. I encourage you to persevere.

Public Speaking

First, recognize that when you make a public presentation, no matter how minor, you will probably get nervous. This is completely normal even for experienced speakers. The nervousness usually passes within a minute or two after you start. Expect it to happen and do not let it shake you. Second, there are three questions you need to ask yourself when preparing to speak. First, ask what it is you want/need to communicate: What is your BIG IDEA. That might seem obvious but I assure you clarity at this point will help you to achieve your goal. Second, understand your audience. The more you know about your audience the better you will be able to find a common point for conveying your message in a way that can be heard and understood. Third, ask how you can communicate your message so it really is heard. One thing is almost certain, communication probably will not happen just by stating the facts. Good communicators match the audience with the right kind of delivery that might be a story, an image, an action, a demonstration, statistics, etc. Never lose sight of the goal to have your audience "get" your message.

Think Before You Criticize

One of the easiest and most practiced habits is to be critical. It is easy to find fault with situations, organizations, and especially other people. It is easy to spew forth our observations, pointing out each fault in detail. Easy, but usually non-productive and more often than not, counter-productive, damaging relationships and creating animosity. Before you criticize others, either to their face or to someone else, stop and think about how you would have handled the situation given the same information and limitations. Odds are you probably would not have done much better, or even as well. The one advantage you may have is experience, which is a good foundation for mentoring and coaching when things do not turn out right. You will get farther, and build a better working relationship, by being full of grace rather than being constantly critical. People who are constantly critical and complaining are unpleasant to be around and limit their own career. Those who respond with grace and understanding have a better chance of making a positive impact, benefit from more fulfilling relationships, and are more likely to advance.

Principle of Life
Resilience

"It doesn't matter what happens to you, what truly matters is how you respond to what happens to you." The stories of those who have overcome adversity to achieve great results inspire us. Yet, somehow, when WE are the ones in adversity the real temptation is to make all kinds of excuses why we should be pitied and excused for quitting. That was not the attitude of Bethany Hamilton who had her arm bitten off by a shark but went on to win 1st place in the Explorer Women's Division of the NSSA National Championships. She is only one of many who are RESILIENT. Do an internet search for: "People who have overcome adversity" and you will find some interesting reading. How resilient are *YOU*? If you have not figured it out already, bad thing happen to everybody--even good people. Bad things will happen to you, perhaps because of your own actions, but sometimes for no reason at all, and completely unexpectedly. Will you allow yourself to be defined by what has happened or will you trust God and move forward. Yes, this is also called making lemonade out of lemons.

Great Followers Make the Best Leaders

This seems obvious, but you cannot really be a great leader until you have learned how to be a great follower. There are several types of followers: the actively disengaged, the slacker, the confronter, the "yes" man and the fully engaged. Each one has specific characteristics; however, it is the fully engaged Follower who rises to become the great Leader. The fully engaged follower is in harmony with the mission and sees a connection between his/her service and the fulfillment of the mission. The fully engaged follower believes his/her contribution makes a difference. If you need an example of a fully engaged follower, think of Jesus. You might be tempted to think, "I'll start giving my 100% when I get into that position of leadership." Alternatively, "Once they start showing me some respect and appreciation, THEN I'll start putting forth my best effort." Obviously, this was not the attitude of Jesus, nor what he expects from those who are called by his name (Christian). Give your best in the position where you find yourself and God will take care of the rest.

(Your Proverb)

Leading Change

If you are in any position of leadership, at some point you will find yourself being responsible for leading a change initiative. It might be something small within a department, or for the entire organization. Change management is a normal part of leadership, but it can be far more complicated than it appears on the surface. Key to effective change is four things. First, before you can implement change you need to have a clear picture of what and where you are going. Too many times people only know they want a change but have not taken the time to identify WHAT they would like in place of the current situation. Second, change will not happen unless there is a sense of urgency. That means a belief that if change does not take place something negative will happen, or something significant will be missed. A sense of urgency is the number one reason why change efforts fail. Third, the change must be fully supported by leadership. Leadership must commit to the change effort in visible and tangible ways, not just words. Fourth, communicate, communicate, and communicate. Under communication is perceived as lack of resolve. If any of these points are absent, your change effort will likely fail.

Scorpion and the Frog

Do you know the story of the Scorpion and the Frog? This is from Aesop's fables. The gist of the story is that a frog agrees to take a scorpion on his back across a flooded river. Half way across, the scorpion stings the frog and they both drown. When the frog asks with his dying breath "why?" the scorpion responds, "it's my nature." You can "google it" and find the full story. The moral of the story is that a scorpion is a scorpion, even when it tries to be, or promises to be, something else. People *can* change…..but it does not happen often and personalities rarely change. God does work miracles and the grace of God does change people. However, also God designed us in the womb to have the personality we have. Everyone deserves to be trusted, but when someone proves untrustworthy, be careful about continuing to trust, *even if they promise that they have changed*. This is definitely a time when the proof is in the pudding. A little paranoia is warranted when dealing with such people and can keep you from falling prey to a scorpion. Trust has to be earned.

Social Media

You possibly have a social media account of some kind; Facebook, Instagram, Twitter, Pininterest, SnapChat, etc. Interacting on social media can be a positive experience and has potential to widen your area of influence. What is bad is not being able to discern what to share, and what to keep private. Keep this in mind: What you share will be available FOREVER. Here is a good rule of thumb: *Never use social media to complain about your job, your boss, your spouse, or your loved ones.* It may feel good to vent, but it will almost certainly have a negative impact on your relationships. Your presence in any social media outlet should be edifying and show a level of maturity. Even personal reflections that are too candid can and probably will come back to haunt you, perhaps blocking you from a job or other opportunities. For those kind of comments get a friend to talk to, but do not spill your guts on social media. I personally have known people who were terminated because of their inappropriate remarks on social media and others who were passed over in the hiring process for the same reason.

Language of RESPECT

Develop a language of respect. Everyone deserves respect, but often the words we choose do not *show* respect. In fact, the words we use often create barriers or close off opportunities. Developing a language of respect requires us to consider how another person will receive our choice of words. Words that are part of a language of respect include "thank you," "you are welcome," "I appreciate," "could you," "would you," "please," "consider," "help me," etc. A language of respect is more than the words, however. It is also the tone of voice and the body language used. Even positive words can have a negative and disrespectful connotation when conveyed with a sarcastic tone or by rolling your eyes in patronization or contempt. Being able to speak in a language of Respect is the height of emotional intelligence. You do this by putting yourself in the other person's place and hearing the words you say as if they were spoken to you. How would you feel? What response do the words generate in you at a gut level? At first this takes a little time, but the more you practice the better you will become.

Be Considerate of Others

Here is a shock: not everything is all about YOU. I know that this may come as a surprise. You may feel as if you are the center of the universe, but it simply is not true. Every indication is that the context of LIFE has everything to do with RELATIONCHIPS, and relationships, by definition, includes others. If there was one life lesson you simply MUST get, it is this fact: All of life can be reduced to relationships. The quality of those relationships hinges upon your awareness of the fact that, 1) YOU are not the center, and 2) the way you *treat* others IS the center. This means more than just being considerate of their feelings. It means to be considerate of their needs and rights as a human being, created in the image of God. I see a lot of inconsiderate behavior by people who think that life IS all about them, giving no thought to how their actions, words, and attitude affect others. Being considerate is a lifestyle of choice. It is not automatic, even for Christians. We *choose* to accept that everything comes down to relationships, which, in turn, is the truest reflection of Christ in our lives. Philippians 2:3 is a good guide for effective living.

Right

Most people would say they know, and do, the "right" thing. However, to say you can be trusted to do the "right" thing is meaningless without a standard. After all, what does "right" mean? All you are really saying is that you will do what *feels* appropriate to you at that moment based on your perception of "right." The true standard of what is "right" can be found in the Bible, and has to do with a complex blend of honesty, commitment, love, humility, justice, holiness and sacrifice. As leaders, we are called upon to do the right thing, but you will not recognize what that is unless you first seek God's standard. That is only half the story. Even when we acknowledge a standard of "right," our behavior is governed by our own needs, greed, and desires. Can you be trusted to do the "right" thing, even when doing so results in consequences that are uncomfortable? Therefore, knowing what is right, and doing what is right are two different things. Righteous living combines both into a life of exemplary character. Proverbs 21:2 states, "People may be right in their own eyes, but the Lord examines their heart."

(Your Proverb)

Gossip

Gossip is the weapon of an assassin targeting relationships. Gossip is the elevation of ME ahead of WE. Gossip is the destroyer of that which God values most: relationships. Those who gossip deal in a narcotic that, in the short term, makes themselves feel better, but in the long term destroys their own peace and joy. For those who gossip, it also says that you cannot be trusted with any information of a sensitive nature. The reason people engage in gossiping is that it makes them feel better about themselves; when they put others down they seem higher by comparison, but that is only an illusion. This is a trick of the devil and comes out of a root of pride within us. Proud that we are smart enough to see the faults of others, and proud that we are better than they are. Sadly, this kind of "feeling good" is an illusion that is never satisfied. It also ignores the fact that we, too, are human with our own weaknesses and failings. Let us go with this: "If it is not nice, necessary, or kind, then don't say anything at all." Remember, all of life can be reduced to relationships and the quality of those relationships influences every area of our lives.

Self-Sabotage

Sabotage is setting into place forces, usually concealed, which lead to destruction. Self-sabotage is the setting into place forces, which lead to my own failure. Self-sabotage is usually unconscious. It occurs when I behave in a way that undermines, or totally blocks, my ability to reach my goals. An example is the woman on her third marriage, who continues to choose husbands who are abusive, even though her goal is a warm healthy relationship. This type of behavior is MUCH more common that you might think, because it flows from our un-reflected experiences. That is, you have experienced something that connects with some aspect of your self-image. We tend to repeat that experience again and again without thinking. This pattern will continue until you take the time to stop and reflect on whether the experience was good or bad and WHY. You can avoid self-sabotage by examining your life, particularly the failures or weak points, and look for patterns. Once you spot them, work backward to discover the behavior(s) that needs to be addressed. Self-sabotage can undermine your entire life, but you can change your inclination to self-sabotage as you become more emotionally intelligent.

Taking Care of Business

Marc LeBlanc, an author and consultant says "Done is better than Perfect." Larry the Cable Guy, a comedian, is known for his "Git'r done" catch phrase. Stephen Covey says, "The main thing is to keep the main thing the main thing." My phrase is "taking care of business." Regardless of how you say it, getting the job done is the point; do the job "right," but keep in mind that "right" and perfect are not the same thing. If you are waiting for things to be perfect before taking action, e.g. submitting an assignment, or turning in a project, you will never get anything done; nothing is ever perfect. There is always a balance between excellence and action. There is always a cost-to-time ratio that has to be considered. Leaders know how to find that balance. If you have a perfectionistic personality, this can be VERY challenging, and often results in quitting, since perfection seems impossible. The first step is to recognize that *Done is better than Perfect.* The second is to make sure that what is done, is done "right" even if not perfect. Take care of business; get the job done and move on.

Time Management

Poor time management is the downfall of many a leader. The ability to understand the difference between the important and everything else can be challenging. Couple that with the pressure of the urgent and you will often find an individual who is literally swamped with work, but accomplishing little. David Horsager suggests you plan your day the night before by identifying the top 5 tasks that are the most important to accomplish, and then making sure those get done first when you come in the next day. Prioritize the rest of your tasks by ranking them 1-10 for importance and 1-10 for urgency. Add the totals and do those with the highest scores first. All of this pre-supposes you are working from a written list of tasks. Anyone who tries to operate from a list in their head (i.e., not written down) will seriously limit their effectiveness and their growth. The ability to effectively manage your time is a KEY skill for any leader. Even more, not being able to do so will limit not only your effectiveness now, but also your ability to advance in your career. YOU HAVE TO MASTER THIS SKILL.

Complacency

Complacency is not the same thing as trust or faith; do not get confused at this point. Trust is an active emotion that builds upon past performance and projects future behavior. Similarly, faith hinges upon belief in people or information that is often unsupported. Both are dynamic and provide foundations for change. Complacency, however, is the acceptance of the status quo at a level that relinquishes any personal options for change; like a piece of driftwood floating on the ocean. Complacent people have become fully assimilated by the culture and their circumstances. They stand for nothing, and accomplish little. They have no passion and never consider the future. While *initiative* is a word that defines leaders, complacent people do not even know the definition of the word. Complacency is a disease that undermines spiritual connection and personal accomplishment. A disease that sinks the individual in a quagmire of apathy and derails individuals, churches, and businesses of purpose and productivity. Like the lotus-eaters of the Odyssey, those who are complacent sleep away in peaceful apathy.

Wisdom

In the Bible book of Proverbs, Solomon writes, "Blessed is the man who finds wisdom, the man who gains understanding" (3:13). The book of Proverbs is Solomon's manual on wisdom. According to Solomon, the wisest man who ever lived, the foundation of wisdom is clearly identified: "The fear of the Lord is the beginning of knowledge" (1:7a). For "fear" in this context read "awe". Until we realize how awesome God is, and whom we are in comparison, true wisdom will be an illusion. All real wisdom starts from that point. Wise people seek wisdom; foolish people believe they are already wise. Seeking wisdom is a purposeful act of humbly seeking instruction. You can choose to learn (wise), or you can believe you already know enough (foolish). Choosing the path of wisdom means always growing, always expanding, and requires a longing on our part to reach our full potential. Gaining wisdom is the passion of any true leader. Therefore, read good books that inspire, listen to lectures & podcasts that enlighten. Engage in discussions that challenge you. Emerge from the cocoon of ignorance; seek wisdom.

(Your Proverb)

Beware Precedent

Precedent is the small vine growing through the seam of concrete that eventually breaks the slab. Precedent is the small root that eventually grows to fill and close off the drainpipe, causing problems and damage. Precedent is ANY decision you make that runs contrary to policy. Precedent will open the door for that decision to happen again, and again. Many times this happens because you want to be nice, or perhaps to avoid confrontation. Both of those reasons are not *compelling* reasons to not follow policy. Yes, there are exceptions to the rule, but they should be supported by a clear and compelling rationale that you can defend. Even with that rationale, precedent will seek to take hold. The moment you make an exception to your policies, you are effectively opening yourself to criticism of favoritism, and possibly even legal action. Do not knee jerk a decision that overrides policy. Think carefully about the policy and that for which it was intended. Consider why you would make an exception, and whether or not that should be part of the policy, or if the policy itself is still viable – not all policies should live forever.

You're Gonna Serve Somebody

Bob Dylan, a singer and musician, in one of his songs says" you're gonna serve somebody, it maybe the Lord, it maybe the Devil, but you're gonna serve somebody". He is right on target: you are serving somebody whether you know it or not. This is an unavoidable fact. Joshua from the Old Testament said to the nation of Israel after they entered the Promised Land. "Chose you this day whom you will serve but as for me and my house we will serve the Lord". *To refuse to choose does not mean you have not chosen.* There are other situations that have the same kind of clear dichotomy, e.g. you can choose to breathe . . . or not. You might want to argue a middle ground, as agnostics are inclined to do. Alternatively, you could suggest an alternate "higher power." However, Acts 4:12 clearly identifies the way to salvation through the name of Jesus. Without a conscious choice to serve God, you are set by default into service of the Devil. This is what I encourage you to do -- Choose to make Jesus the Lord of your Life. In him, you will find the fullness of what you were meant to be. Any other path will leave you empty and ultimately lost.

Juggling

I am not talking about actually juggling physical items, e.g. bowling pins, instead, I am referencing the ability to keep more than two projects (or activities within a single project) moving forward. The more projects/activities you are able to keep moving forward, the more you will be able to accomplish, and the higher you have the potential to rise. As I have mentioned before, this is not multitasking (since humans cannot really multitask). It is effective task shifting. Not all projects/activities are the same size or of equal importance. Therefore, when learning to juggle, it is crucial that you identify which projects or activities are the most important. Clarify the timelines for delivering progress, and make sure to meet those deadlines. Also, recognize some projects/activities are more time consuming than others and take more time to keep in the air. Sometimes the larger projects/activities are not as important, but because they are large they give the impression of being important, and failing could be potentially more costly to your credibility. To mix metaphors, it is a balancing act. Leaders have to be able to juggle.

Compartmentalize

To compartmentalize means to be able to take all the mental baggage of an issue, put it into a room or compartment in your mind, and then close the door so that you can focus upon another issue. This is similar to juggling, but it differs in that usually the issues that need to be compartmentalized have the potential of completely de-railing your entire focus, and negatively affecting your life. For example, if you have a major personal issue that could affect your performance at work, being able to compartmentalize it will allow you to stay engaged at work. The ability to compartmentalize requires emotional intelligence and self-discipline. When you intentionally practice compartmentalization, you become more productive, because you have enhanced your ability focus. An interesting book: *Men are like Waffles – Women are Like Spaghetti*, by Bill and Pam Ferrell, suggests that men may be better at this than women may. I am not sure that is true, but I know it is a valuable skill. However, there is a dark side to watch out for: compartmentalization can also be a way to escape from a reality you do not want to face.

Urgency

What a great word… and what an overlooked emotion and tool. Rather, I should say an emotion/tool often misapplied in our lives, which creates stress but accomplishes little. We are busy, very busy, without an understanding of what urgency is really about. Urgency is all about achieving success, no matter the area of life. Being urgent about the right things can generate and sustain change; it can facilitate strategic accomplishment. Being urgent about the wrong things generates busy people who accomplish next to nothing. Leaders understand the importance of creating a sense of urgency for their organization. If you can create a sense of urgency connected to your business or product, and couple that with strategic vision and execution, you can achieve success. If you cannot generate a sense of urgency, then all the strategic planning in the world will not help you achieve your goals. Without a sense of urgency *focused on the right things*, apathy and eventually failure are the norm. Urgency is the difference between success and mediocrity.

Adversity

Adversity always seems to come at an unexpected time, from an unexpected source, or both. Even when you know it is coming, it can throw you off. However, you can prepare yourself, to some degree ahead of time. Here is how: cast yourself fully upon Jesus. A.W. Tozer stated: When I understand that everything happening to me is to make me more Christ like, it resolves a great deal of anxiety." Trust in *Him* with ALL your heart. Believe He is in control even when you cannot see a way out. This allows for peace in the storm, even though you will still get wet! Everything else results in stress and anxiety. This kind of trust requires practice. This is called faith, and that is the stumbling stone upon which many will fall, because it sounds impossible. That being said, adversity, no matter how well you are prepared, or the depth of your faith, may still cause heartache and strong emotions. Even Jesus wept at the loss of a friend. Faith does not mean you will not grieve, feel betrayed or get angry. Accept your emotions as part of the process, and then come back to the strong foundation of faith. God is in control and He does have a plan for your life.

(Your Proverb)

Sustainability

Sustainability is when a process or action can be repeated reliably and efficiently. A sustainable solution is one that is conceived in urgency, birthed by being clearly communicated, and nurtured by leadership until it is part of the culture. The advantage of sustainability is that, once the process is clearly understood and implemented, it can run with minimal supervision, freeing leadership to focus on other areas. Any decision which results in a process that is too cumbersome will eventually be ignored, and the process fail: it is not sustainable. Sustainability requires the intentional effort of leadership to a) clearly communicate the need, b) clearly communicate the process/change/solution, and c) keep on communicating support for the process/change/solution until is it firmly grounded in the corporate culture. This is where most processes break down; being grounded in the culture. Without this grounding sustainability is an illusion that will fade as soon as the leader focuses on the next task. Creating sustainability by firmly grounding the process in the culture is the genius of great leaders.

Technology

This, like so much else, requires balance. I saw a commercial on television where a new driver had a flat tire. He called his father who was instructing him on how to change the tire. His father asked if he knew what a tire iron was. The young man answered yes in an uncertain voice, while holding up a different tool. It was easy to see he was clueless. Here is where the balance comes in, you may not choose to change the tire yourself, but you should know the tools in case you have to. That is the same with technology. You will likely never be familiar with all the aspects of technology which are available to you or which your company uses, but, there are certain aspects of technology which cannot be ignored without potential negative repercussions. It is unacceptable for a leader in our society to be completely technophobic. There is simply too much to be gained by leveraging technology effectively. By avoiding a working knowledge of technology, you place yourself at the mercy of those who are conversant in technology and dependent upon them to provide you accurate and reliable information.

Grace, Mercy & Accountability

Grace is unmerited *favor* or kindness; for instance, when you do something nice for someone for no reason at all you are being gracious. Mercy is unwarranted *forgiveness*, or at the very least, unwarranted forbearance. Accountability is the process whereby an individual is held responsible, to an expectation. Let us face it, finding the right balance in showing grace and mercy, while holding people accountable can be challenging. Here are some guidelines that I use in finding that balance: 1. Make sure expectations are clear. 2. Always attempt to be gracious 3. If there is genuine remorse expressed by an individual who has missed the mark, then I try to err on the side of mercy. 4. However, if the problem persists or, if there is not any, or only insincere, remorse, reinforce the expectation with an appropriate discipline. Granting mercy in these cases can actually enable poor performance and bad behavior. While there is a place for grace and mercy, there is also a place for "tough love" and accountability. People always do better when, as their leader, you can find the right balance.

Are you Shouting?

There is a place for shouting and raised voices, for instance, Boot Camp, or perhaps the athletic training field. One place where shouting is not acceptable is the office. If you, as the leader, are shouting at your people, then it probably is not the employee that has the problem-- it is you. You need to get control of your emotions and demonstrate some discipline. "But," you say, "I'm just passionate or that's just the way I am, and everybody knows it." Both of these could be true, but neither are an adequate excuse for a blatant lack of emotional control. On the other hand, you might say, "That employee has made a mistake which will cost the company a lot of money to fix." Again, this could be true, but shouting at the employee does not fix the problem. Such behavior is abusive, and not appropriate in an office setting. I have witnessed some executives purposefully employing this tactic in an effort to cower or manipulate an employee, or to reinforce a point. In my opinion, this always makes me think less of the executive. Emotional control is the hallmark of great leaders, even the passionate ones!

The Greatest is Love

At the end of 1 Corinthians 13, Paul identifies 3 things that should be a part of our lives: faith, hope, and love. These attitudes/actions/characteristics form the core of a fulfilled life, and even more importantly, a life that is pleasing to God. Paul concludes the chapter by saying, "but the greatest of these is love." In context, it is easy to understand that what he means is that we should show love in all our interactions, not just toward the people we like or the ones we know. EVERYBODY! When we do this, we have achieved a level of maturity and fulfillment. It is interesting that secular writers and thinkers repeat this theme often. From the Beatles', "all you need is love, love, love is all you need," to Joel Manby's book for business leaders: *Love Works*, where he states, "Love isn't a feeling, but an action, an action by which leaders and entire organizations can experience almost unimaginable success *and* personal fulfillment" (p.22). These are only two examples I am sure you can think of many others. Bottom line: Make love your operational philosophy.

Take Care of Business

Many people imagine the leader in a business as the one giving orders, but not seeming to do any of the hard work themselves. Wrong! Real leaders are hard workers who take of business. If something needs doing, they make sure it is done, even if they have to do it themselves. If a job needs an extra pair of hands, they jump in with a willing, positive attitude. Leaders are not afraid of hard work, and actually embrace the reality that great things only come about through hard work. They lead from the front and set an example for those who follow. "Taking care of business" is an attitude. Those who have this attitude are often called "doers" because they "do"; that is, they do not wait to be told what to do, or wait around for someone else to act; they act. While there can be some negatives associated with this attitude, the positives far outweigh any negatives. Those with this attitude are treasures in any organization. They accomplish more in less time than most other individuals, often as much as two or three others, all with a better attitude and less complaining. You can adopt this attitude yourself, simply chose to act.

(Your Proverb)

Self-Pity

Self-pity is a normal emotional response whenever you feel like you are a victim. That can happen for any number of reasons, many, if not most, of them seem justified. This is important: *Self Pity has the effect of lowering your defenses to temptation, making it easier for you to rationalize behavior that you would normally avoid.* You will always be faced with temptation, but under normal circumstances, you are probably able to resist. However, when you perceive yourself to be the victim, particularly when you feel whatever has happened to you is undeserved, your ability to resist temptation is diminished. Your brain begins to contrive of reasons why it is okay for you to yield to temptation "this one time," how you deserve a special exception in this one case, since what happened to you was undeserved and so bad. MAKE NO MISTAKE, THIS WILL HAPPEN TO YOU! The first step to overcoming this temptation is to recognize what is driving it, that is, your feeling sorry for yourself. The second step is to divert your attention away from the temptation. Remember, resist the devil and he will flee from you.

Default Mode

By Default Mode, I mean how you are programed to react or behave. Personality is part of this but, this programming also is affected by a combination of your DNA and how you were raised, including the influences upon you as you were growing up. The BIG question is, "Do you know your Default Mode of response?" and "Are you satisfied with it?" Most people never give any thought to this, and are trapped by their programing in self-defeating patterns of behavior. Understanding yourself and your Default Mode response gives you the opportunity to make adjustments. Changing your programing can be accomplished, but it requires disciplined effort over a long period. Changing your internal programing can be derailed by stress, weariness, and negative experiences, which open the door for temptation to return to the old default mode. Start by focusing on one aspect of your Default Mode response, e.g. being defensive. Reflect back over your day and identify when you have exhibited that response, then begin to focus on catching yourself in the act. Once you do that you can begin to change that response.

The Brutal Truth

This topic comes from Jim Collins' book *Good to Great*, which you should read if you have not already. Being able, and willing, to confront the brutal truth is one of the most important lessons of leadership. Mostly what leaders hear, and what they want to hear, is that things are going well and the company is prospering. If that can't be said, then the next best thing is to find an external excuse, preferably one that is out of anyone's direct control, like the economy the weather, society values, etc. upon which to blame any negative news. *Almost no one wants to confront the brutal truth about lack of progress and/or roadblocks in achieving a goal*, which is why mediocrity is the norm. Because of this, problems are almost never addressed unless they become impossible to ignore. The more you know about what is *really* happening, the better you will be in a position to adapt and flow with the changes necessary to succeed. The more you hide behind good news and "yes" men, the more likely you are to crash and burn. Confronting the brutal truth requires a willingness to seek out and demand the hard facts, even if unpleasant.

Eye Contact

The act of looking someone in the eye and holding that look, while sharing from the heart, can be a powerful and persuasive force. Those who are master communicators understand and practice this tactic whenever they are intent on influencing you to their point of view. This can be done in a public speaking format, targeting a few people scattered in the audience, or it can be in a one-on-one conversation. It is in the one-on-one conversation where the real force of this tactic becomes evident, where the true power of can be felt. When making eye contact, there are two things to keep in mind: 1. Look directly in the other individual's eye for at least 1-2 solid seconds, and come back to their eyes frequently over the duration of the conversation for at least a second. 2. Be sure you are being genuine and telling the truth. Your passion and commitment should be evident in your manner and tone of voice. This tactic generates influence and buy-in. However, if you use this to lie or manipulate, it will ultimately destroy trust and ruin your relationship.

Pick up the PHONE!!!!

I know we live in a digital age. I know that we depend on email and text messages for almost all of our communication, not to mention LinkedIN, Facebook, Twitter, Pinterest, Snapchat, Instagram, etc. In most cases, these forms of communication are entirely adequate to get a message across. In fact, these forms of communication can be extremely effective because they leave a nice digital trail to refer back to if necessary. They also allow for a thought-out response and the ability to articulate both the problem and resolution in terms that make understanding better. However, there are still times when nothing beats a phone call. If you are emailing/texting/etc. back and forth on an issue more than three times, *just pick up the phone!* If you have a real urgency in getting a response, just pick up the phone! Don't allow or accept failing in meeting a responsibility simply because someone won't respond to your digital communication, pick up the phone, or even better, if possible, walk over to where they are working and talk to them in person.

Respect, Honor, & Love

I was listening to a speaker once, who said, "Men are fueled by honor and respect, while women are fueled by love". I have noticed that men do indeed respond better when they feel they are being treated with respect and honor; this applies to the home, the workplace and social gatherings. When we intentionally treat the men in our lives with respect and honor, they are more likely to live up to those expectations and be men who deserve respect and honor. Respect an honor are conveyed in choice of words, body language, and attitude. Each of these components are important in the overall message. The speaker's intent when stating that women should be treated with love means an appropriate type of love, for example, as toward a sister or mother. Perhaps a better way to state this, in the context of our society, is to treat women as being valued for who they are. When women are treated as being valued for themselves they, are more likely to live up to that high standard. In both cases, we are treating people as God would have us to; as people made in His image, and so are fulfilling the will of God. This results in a happier and more fulfilling life for everybody.

(Your Proverb)

Triangles

Triangles, in terms of relationships, has to do with the distribution of power and manipulation. If you are in conflict with someone, the best resolution comes when you deal with that person, and work out the problem directly. A triangle happens when you go to someone else *within the same network* and present your case in order to get him or her on your side and get their help in influencing a decision in your favor. When the triangled person is persuaded to act, without all of the facts, based only on your side of the story and your personal relationship, that is where problems occur and the situation escalates. After, all there are always two sides to any story. If you are approached and asked to take a side, DO NOT agree until you have heard the other side of the story. You can be supportive without escalating a problem. Either recommend the person trying to get you on their side to handle it personally, or offer to sit down with all parties together to work it out. NEVER commit to a course of action until you get the full story. People under duress often neglect to mention details that cast themselves or their situation in a bad light.

Politics

No, this proverb is not about politics as it is usually discussed. Politics, when boiled down to its essence, is about the structure and functioning of relationships for the mutual benefit of all, usually through laws, policies, or procedures. Realistically, whenever there are human relationships, you also have politics; the two are inseparable. The more people involved, the greater the significance of politics. Of course, people, being people, twist what is supposed to be for the mutual benefit of all, to the sole benefit of themselves. Leaders must understand and accept that politics are unavoidable. Wise leaders will embrace a knowledge of politics and develop the skills necessary to work with people to achieve the goals of the organization. Those who choose to ignore or complain about the existence of political considerations demonstrate their own ignorance of how we are created. As you can no doubt see from watching our governmental politicians, not everyone agrees on what is in the mutual benefit of all. That does not change the reality of the existence of politics, it just emphasizes the complexity.

Stay in your Box

I have a friend whose mantra is, "stay in your box." By that he means to focus on your own area and do not be sidetracked into other areas which are not your responsibility. From one perspective, this is solid advice. The more you focus on your own work, the more likely you are to be able to complete your tasks with excellence. From another perspective, it can be a career killer. If you become the very best in your "box" but never take an interest in other areas, assisting or contributing for improvement, you may find that it becomes nearly impossible to break out of that "box." That "box" becomes your definition. The better you are at your job and in your "box," the more indispensable you become in that position, and the less likely you are to be thought of as someone who has other skills or capabilities. So, show some interest in other areas within your organization. Offer your assistance to your colleagues when able. Discuss strategies for improvements within your area, and the organization as a whole, and you will find your horizons broadening.

Family can drive you Crazy!

This seems to be a universal truth! Family members will irritate, annoy, and just generally rub you the wrong way - sometimes. Parents will nag, siblings will snipe, and children will whine, all of it with some seemingly grand conspiracy to drive you crazy. For me that is a relatively short drive anyway. It is not just you or your family, it happens to all of us. Nevertheless, and here is the important thing to keep in mind, at other times they support you, defend you, and encourage you. Try to keep things in perspective. Accept that there will be the crazy times, and enjoy the good times. Your ability to appreciate the ebb and flow of family comes as you begin to realize that you are a participant in *driving them crazy*, just as they do to you. You, like them, are part of the problem and part of the solution. The more you learn self-control the better you will be able to put it all in perspective. That is right; their craziness is overcome *not by them changing* but by you getting better control of yourself, particularly your tongue. A lot of things that you could say probably do not need to be said! What you say has the power to increase or decrease the craziness.

Expediency, Exigency, & Ethics

Ethics: that branch of philosophy dealing with values relating to human conduct, with respect to the rightness and wrongness of certain actions and their motives.

Expediency: a regard for what is politically correct or personally advantageous regardless of whether or not it is ethically correct.

Exigency: need, demand, or requirement based on the urgency of circumstances and the immediate situation without regard to ethical considerations.

I think it is accurate to state that most of us would say that we live our lives according to an ethical standard. That standard includes such moral virtues as honesty, respect, fairness, etc. Yet, the Ethical conduct of our life is constantly under pressure to bend to the needs of Exigency and Expediency. Three 'E' words that make all the difference in how we live and conduct our lives. It is better to live right, and to choose right in advance of exigency than to allow expediency to prevail and push you into actions opposed to your values. If you are not careful, exigency and expediency will derail your ethics. Know your core values and stand fast.

Mission Statement

As you know, most organizations have a Mission Statement; this includes for-profits, not-for-profits, churches, etc. The mission statement defines what the organization has established as its reason for existing. It often contains language that focuses the organization's activities toward a particular market niche, or upon a product type. For example, "Our company exists to provide high quality electronic parts for the automotive industry." The benefits of the mission statement are that it clarifies what the company DOES and does NOT do, which allows greater ability to focus on quality on the things you do. People can have mission statements, too. A personal mission statement clarifies why YOU exist. It provides boundaries in your life that can be very useful in keeping your focus on the goals you have for your life. Mission Statements must be dynamic, by that I mean that a mission statement's value is in its active guidance in your life. Simply having a mission statement if it does not influence your choices and lifestyle is meaningless. Take some time to ponder this and write out a mission statement for yourself.

(Your Proverb)

How to Treat Each Other

First Timothy 5:1-2 states: "Do not rebuke an older man harshly, but exhort him as if he were you father. Treat younger men as brothers, older women as mothers, and younger women as sisters, with absolute purity." This passage resonates with the ramifications of "being created in the image of God." We all hold this in common, regardless of race or creed. Treating any person in a way that demeans or disrespects them, damages our own personhood. When you understand that everything can be reduced to relationships, our interactions with others has the power to elevate us closer to the image of the One who created us, or distorts that image, which lessens our humanity. When we treat everyone one as we ourselves would like to be treated, it reflects our love for God and appreciation for his grace and mercy. That is why I think Timothy's statement above is so important, because it focuses on the importance of relationships using the analogy of family. When we see others as part of our own family, we had better grasp the significance of what we say and do.

Leadership types

Bob Whitsel in "Preparing for Change" states that there are not only leadership styles, there are also leadership types. These leadership types are much more a part of who you are and are less changeable than leadership styles. Although you likely have a default leadership *style*, you can you change that style of leadership to fit the circumstances, or the individuals, you are leading, but not so much your *type* of leadership. Below are the basic types. I encourage you to check out his book for more information. Making peace with who you are can unleash great possibilities.

- Strategic Leaders - they see steps 1 and 5 but struggle with steps 2, 3, and 4.
- Tactical Leaders - they see steps 2, 3, and 4 and can work with the how to get them done efficiently and effectively. Strategic leaders NEED Tactical leaders to realize their vision.
- Process Leaders - they refine the processes for greater efficiency and functionality.
- Operational Leaders - they foster teamwork, creativity and unity toward a goal.

Good vs. Great

Jim Collins in his classic book "*Good to Great*," states, "good is the enemy of great." He goes on to explain that most people get to the level of "good" in almost any aspect of their personal or professional life, and then tend to slow down on their efforts to improve. There is a sense in some situations where "good enough" truly is good enough, and continued efforts can result in non-productive results. I believe strongly in putting forth excellence in all things, but I also realize that sometimes excellence is accepting the "good" and moving forward. However, there is also a time and place for striving for "great." Getting to great in anything requires a persevering spirit that does not settle for "good enough." Great requires disciplined effort and focus. Achieving great demands more of everything and everyone: more work, more discipline, more sacrifice, more practice, more resources, etc. When an individual or an organization is willing to put in the *more*, then the results can be extraordinary. Carefully consider your life goals and whether or not "good" is good enough, or if you are willing to pay the price for "great."

Get in the right seat

Jim Collins in his book, *Good to Great* talks about the importance of matching your skills and interests with your work. He uses the metaphor of a bus to illustrate the importance of aligning with the right organization, and finding the right place within the organization. His metaphor has been used my many to talk about "getting on the right bus," i.e. make sure you are aligned with an organization or institution which matches your values. Add to that is the discussion focused on making sure, as a leader, that the individuals within the organization are in the "right seat" on the bus, i.e. that they are in a position to reach their fullest potential. People, who may be exceptionally gifted in one area, but work in another, often find their productivity diminished, and their satisfaction low. However, when you can match your skills/interests with your work, that is, getting in the right seat on the bus, you can see amazing results. To do this requires you to stop and ask yourself if you are in the right seat in the bus (or even on the right bus!). If you cannot answer yes, then to start thinking about what that should look like, and then go for it.

Find the Balance

You may have walked across a balance beam as a young person, or perhaps across a log stretching between the banks of a stream or gully. When we were growing up my brother and I would walk across a log over an empty streambed, but when we got to the middle we would do whatever we could to get the other one to fall off. I learned quickly that, while it takes balance even to get across the log, when you are faced with challenges, keeping your balance can be much harder. If you struggled simply to get across the log, you stood almost no chance when someone else is bouncing up and down on the log and it starts to sway underneath you! I've no doubt that you probably have already felt as if the "log" you are standing on is bouncing and swaying and you may feel as if someone is pushing, trying to get you to fall off. First, do not despair, you are not alone, most of us have felt that way. Second, read Isaiah 40:31 and place your hope in God. Third, if you fall off the log, accept it as a learning experience and GET RIGHT BACK UP on the log. Moment by moment, hour by hour, day by day, you will get to the end if you do not quit.

The Control of the Tongue

The book of James in the Bible, chapter 3:1-12 talks about the control of the tongue. James writes, ""We all stumble in many ways. If anyone is never at fault in what he says, he is a perfect man, able to keep his whole body in check."(v.2) and "no man can tame the tongue. It is a restless evil, full of deadly poison."(v8) There are many other references in the Bible regarding the difficulty in controlling what we say. This is such a common issue that our society has clichés that highlight the problem, like, "think before you speak," or "foot-in-mouth disease," or "stop running your mouth before you swallow your head." The fact of the matter is that the one who can discipline their speech will be considered wise. James also writes in 1:19, "…be quick to listen, slow to speak and slow to become angry." Great advice, because taking some time to think, BEFORE speaking can solve many of the problems unleashed by undisciplined people. Your sharp tongue is not a blessing to anyone, including yourself. Work on focusing your comments to edify and avoid causing unnecessary harm and you will be wise.

(Your Proverb)

Economic Awareness

Pretty much everything comes with a price. That is a truth that is best learned early. Proverbs 21:25 states "Despite their desires, the lazy will come to ruin, for their hands refuse to work." If you do not work, you do not earn wages, and without those wages, you cannot buy food or pay rent or a mortgage. Economics is all about supply and demand. Whatever you desire (demand) has to be met by a limited supply. The more limited the supply, the greater the cost. Although usually only thought of in terms of buying and selling, economics is much broader and touches every area of your life. Nothing is truly *free*, everything comes with a cost of some kind. Everything is connected to supply and demand. Understanding the basics of economics will stand you in good stead throughout your life. Attend a class on economics, read a book on the subject, familiarize yourself with the basic principles, for example, *Economics Through Everyday Life* by Anthony Clark. Familiarity with economic principles will make you more competent, and better able to succeed no matter what you do.

Making conversation

Whether in group of three to five individuals, or simply one-on-one, the ability to engage in conversation is a crucial skill. I say crucial, because this ability is the beginning step in forming a relationship. Almost all relationships have a communication component, verbal or otherwise. Relationships form the foundation of all meaningful human interaction. The best way to develop the skill of conversation is to start from a common point of reference, for instance, sports, the weather, hometowns, cars, etc. Building on that, from a perspective of genuine interest, begin asking questions and sharing from your own experience. Conversation is a two-way street and sharing from your life is an important part of the process. When you bring your genuine interest into this process, amazing things can happen. Not least, is the gift you are giving to another person of your time and interest, which equates to respect. Treating others with respect honors God and all created in his image. So, take a chance and start a conversation; the more you practice this skill the easier it will get. I think you will find yourself blessed as you make the effort.

Generosity

St. Nicholas was noted for his generosity, and out of that grew the giving of gifts at Christmas. He did it as a response to God's love that had been freely given to him. His generous spirit literally changed the world. How will you be remembered? As someone with a generous spirit, or as a scrooge? A spirit of generosity affects every area of our lives: our finances, our time, and our attitude, these being the major areas of application. In finance, take stock of how you respond in simple situations such as giving a tip to a server. Are you carefully calculating the tip down to the penny or remembering that you are affecting a life and leaving a witness? For time, consider how much your own agenda dictates your life. Generous people willingly pause along their path to share of themselves to benefit others. Our impatience with, and harshness toward, others is a reflection of a scrooge mentality. Generosity is the guiding principle for people with heart and passion, and one that refreshes the spirit when practiced.

Posture

You might not think it but when your parents told you to "sit up straight" and "quit slouching," they were doing you a much bigger favor than you imagined. The reason for this is that we form opinions about people in the first three seconds of meeting them. Although not usually part of a conscious process, the awareness of a person's posture and general overall carriage is a strong factor in our first opinions. A person with an upright and erect posture is presenting himself or herself as someone who has a strong sense of personal worth and confidence. Those who slouch give the unconscious message of poor self-esteem, or laziness, or both. A person's general carriage conveys much about a person that is only picked up sub-consciously. You can test this by consciously reflecting on your opinions of others while people watching at the mall or a restaurant. Just by their posture and general carriage alone, describe their general effectiveness. That conscious exercise is repeated subconsciously by you and by others about you, constantly. So, hold your head up and portray the image of yourself you know to be true.

Hire People Smarter Than You

Hiring people who are smarter than you are seems counterintuitive. It seems like, as leader, you should know more than those you employ, about every aspect of the job. That, however, would be wrong, especially in the current age in which we live. Hiring people smarter than you will be difficult if you think you are the smartest person in the room. However, if you can get over yourself, you will soon realize there are many areas where you do not know the answers. Smart leaders hire even smarter workers who can help the organization move forward. This raises the entire ship. Some leaders fear to do this, believing that they will be displaced, so they hire inept followers, who require extra effort in leading to achieve mediocre results, just so they can look important. Be smart. Hire smart people and turn them loose. You will wind up getting the credit for hiring people who make everything better. Hire people smarter than you are, and then do all you can to provide them the resources they need to achieve success. When you do that, the organization succeeds and you will be recognized for providing good leadership.

Apologize

There is very little that is as effective in shutting down criticism as a simple apology. Saying you are sorry, and genuinely meaning it, is a powerful tool real leaders are willing to use in their pursuit of larger goals. If you can say, "I'm sorry" and mean it, and then learn from the experience, your credibility grows, as does your influence. If, instead, you try to cover up your mistakes or blame them on others, or the circumstances, you are effectively giving away your power and weakening your credibility; you are undermining yourself even though you may think you are presenting a strong position. Of course, if you say you are sorry but do not mean it, then any positive benefit from your apology is lost. How can someone tell if you mean it? By not doing or saying the thing again for which you are apologizing now. Repeating the same action, or saying the same thing demonstrates you have no credibility and actually weakens your position, no matter how much you apologize. So next time you make a mistake, take ownership and say, "I'm sorry," and see what happens.

(Your Proverb)

Pride Goes Before a Fall

That is actually a variation of Proverbs 16:18 (from the Bible): "Pride goes before destruction…." Here is another, "Do not think of yourself more highly that you ought…." Romans 12:3. Jim Collins in *Good to Great* described the difference between companies that performed at good levels, and those that could be considered great. Several years later, he wrote a follow-up book titled *How the Mighty Fall*, which described how many of those "great" companies, had crumbled. If you reduced the cause for their fall into one word, it would be PRIDE. While there are positive aspects of pride, such as self-confidence and positive self-worth, when unchecked, it makes us arrogant, pompous, and overly confident. When we begin to think we are someone important, and act as if we have the right to bend laws and rules just because of who we are, we are heading for destruction. Only God is truly great, and His strength is made perfect in our weakness. Adopt an attitude of humility and you just might make a difference. Pride will derail your life, and you may not even notice until too late. Pride goes before a fall.

WIIFM

WIIFM stands for: "What's In It For Me." WIIFM is the operational philosophy of nearly 100% of the population, nearly 100% of the time, including you and me. Yes, there are a LOT of people who say they operate under a different philosophy, and there may be a few who do, at least occasionally, but, by and large, that number is low. Christians strive to operate out of a philosophy of love and consideration of others above self. This is as it should be and God's design, but most give little thought to anyone or anything without first considering the WIIFM, albeit unconsciously. This the theme of one of my most recommended leadership books: *The Greatest Management Principle in the World*, by Michael LeBoeuf. If you can fully grasp the degree to which WIIFM is ingrained in the human spirit, you will have the capacity to be a better communicator, a better friend, and a better leader. While we acknowledge, "it's not all about me," in reality we operate as if it IS all about me. Your ability to understand the WIIFM and apply it puts you miles ahead in understanding relationships and maximizing those relationships in every area of your life.

Blind Spots – Johari Window

The Johari window is a psychological tool that looks at self-awareness, specifically mapping awareness of our idiosyncrasies into a matrix of four blocks:
1) that which is known by others, and ourselves
2) that which others know but we do not know it about ourselves,
3) that which we know about ourselves but others do not know, and
4) that which neither others nor we ourselves know about our personality/behavior.

The reason I include this in a proverb is that self-knowledge is fundamental to wisdom. Thinking about the different blocks in the Johari window, particularly blocks 2 and 4, opens up opportunities for personal growth and improvement. Expanding blocks 1 and 3 is the goal, along with determining where the appropriate line should be between those blocks. Never lose sight of the fact that others may have knowledge about you that you may not possess about yourself. I encourage you to do a little research in this area and expand your self-awareness.

A Little Paranoia is Healthy

A wise person will always understand that things rarely go as planned. Helmuth von Moltke stated, "No battle plan survives contact with the enemy." It is good to have a plan. The sad truth, however, is that as often as not the plan *does not* come together, at least as originally conceived. So, be prepared, at least mentally, for things to go awry. Always keep in mind the very real likelihood that you WILL need a plan 'B,' and perhaps even a plan 'C' and 'D.' This little bit of paranoia will give you the ability to accept reality as it unfolds, and be flexible in modifying the plan as necessary. I do not think anyone starts out with the thought that they will not be able to fulfill their promise and wind up letting you down. I do not think most people plan to say something that effectively "throws you under the bus." The universe is not conspiring for you to fail, but these things happen. With that in mind, do not be surprised when things do not work out as you have planned. Be a little paranoid and always have a plan 'B.' When you can be resilient in the face of unexpected problems you can pull the proverbial rabbit out of the hat and make the impossible possible.

Before You Respond . . .

The normal thing to do when attacked is to respond in kind, or run away. If someone yells at you, the natural inclination is to raise your own voice in response. If someone strikes you, the natural inclination is to strike him or her back. If someone sends you a critical email, the natural inclination is to send back an equally critical email. These are all natural reactions and in almost every case, these are the WRONG reactions. Responding in kind to these kind of stimuli evidences poor emotional intelligence and weak leadership skills. Before you respond, train yourself NOT to respond immediately, until you have had a chance to contemplate an appropriate response. The best way to do this is to take several deep breaths. Doing this does two things, first it provides extra oxygen to your brain, which you need to overcome your hormonal, natural, response reflex, and second, it give you a second or two for the hormones to pass through your system. The next step is to actually think about what was being said/done and try to understand the motive behind the words/actions. Then, you can formulate what an appropriate response should be in light of YOUR personal goals.

In the Moment

Mother Angelica said, "If I'm living in the future or I'm living in the past, I'm not receptive to the grace of the Present Moment." For her, the *Present Moment* took on the importance of a sacrament. As she explains it:

> ...I was getting too caught up in the problems of each day. They would overwhelm me. At that point, I decided I couldn't do that. You handle this moment, then the next, and then you forget about it and move on to the next moment. ...to bear everything that happened today and everything that will happen tomorrow all at one time is too much for anyone. (Mother Angelica's Little Book of Life Lessons and Everyday Spirituality)

Mother Angelica even went so far as to develop a Prayer of the Present Moment. The key to being effective is to be fully present in each moment. Of course you need to be aware of the past, and have a plan for the future, but being able to bring to bear your whole concentration and focus on this moment in time: on this conversation, on this email, on this project, etc., results in higher levels of performance and accomplishment. Training yourself to be in the moment starts with valuing each second as full of opportunity.

(Your Proverb)

Bad Company Corrupts

Paul writes in the book of 1 Corinthians "Bad Company corrupts good character" (15:33). Another saying goes, "one bad apple spoils the whole barrel." Both of these sayings are experiential proverbs that point to the direct connection between who we associate with, and how they influence our behavior. To be more explicit: Your friends are going to have a powerful influence upon your own character and behavior. Some would say this is a perfect opportunity to be a positive influence upon them. Time and experience prove this less likely than their negative behavior influencing you. You may or may not agree, so I will argue from a parental perspective. Regardless of how you choose to allow negative influences into your own life, be as careful as possible to be VERY selective of your children's friends. Those friends can, and will, have an influence upon your children far beyond what you can imagine. They can support them along the path to a bright future, or they can lead them down a path that contains only pain and darkness. Do not ignore this most important role as a parent. Help them by putting them into good company.

Don't Sell Yourself Short

Have you ever noticed that throughout history it is the right person, at the right time, in the right place that has made all the difference? It is true! Not only is the Bible full of examples like that, e.g. Noah, Moses, David, Paul, and many, many others, not the least of which was Esther. In fact, she was at a key point in the history of the Jewish people that was literally life and death for the entire Jewish race across the known world. Her uncle, Mordecai told her "Who knows if perhaps you were made queen for just such a time as this?" Because I know that God has created each person unique and special in His eyes, regardless of the valuation of the world or society, I know that each of us has the potential to be the right person, at the right time, and in the right place to make a difference. Esther's choice to do so was fraught with danger and potential death; I am sure she would have rather someone else stepped forward, but because *she* did, God honored her and delivered her people. God loves you, as amazing as that may be to you. His strength is made perfect in our weakness. Do not accept the value the world wants to place on you, instead step forward knowing that God has your back.

Does Your Stuff Own You?

This may be one of the more difficult proverbs for Americans. After all, the American dream is all about owning stuff. Let me be clear, there is nothing wrong with owning stuff. The problem comes when your stuff begins to own you; when it dictates how you spend your free time and your discretionary money; when that stuff takes the place of God in your life, or detracts from your ability to worship Him with your time or money. When you buy a boat, is the only time when you use it on Sunday, which takes you out of church? Same with a vacation cottage – Does owing that cottage take you out of serving in your local church? Does the money invested in these possessions detract from your ability to tithe? But it is not just about stuff, it can also be about lifestyle. Are you children so involved in sports that you frequently have to miss church? When sports or other social activities come before your public worship of God, what message does that send to your children? When they are grown will their passion for God take a backseat to whatever other activities are going on? It behooves each of us to carefully keep our stuff and our lifestyle in proper perspective.

Credit and YOU

I am embarrassed to admit it, but I allowed myself to fall into credit card debt to the tune of thousands of dollars when I was younger. At first I was so impressed that I qualified for a credit card that it made me feel important that I had it, and powerful when I used it. As I began to see the debt climb, I told myself that I would reserve it for emergencies only, but I found that almost everything could be rationalized as an emergency with the right argument. And then, I thought, I'm disciplined enough, I'll just use the credit card for all my purchases during the month and pay it off at the end, except I spent more than I was making, and the debt grew. It has taken me decades to crawl out from underneath that debt, inch by grueling inch. I would save you that grief, not to mention the thousands of dollars lost to interest. Stay away from credit cards, period. Use a debit card and stay within your budget. It may not be popular, it may mean you will not be able to make some purchases you think you "need," but it will save you much grief and hurtful arguments with those you love. When you get the credit card offers, shred them, before they shred you!

Fight of the two wolves

The story of the two wolves is so often repeated it is hard to determine where it originated. It goes like this. A man is teaching his grandson about life and tells him that he has two wolves fighting inside of him; one is evil and expresses itself in anger, envy, greed, arrogance, bigotry, self-pity, lies, and depravity. The other wolf is good and expresses itself in joy, peace, hope, love, kindness, humility, benevolence, generosity, truth and compassion. The grandson looks at his grandfather and, after considering what he has been told, asks, "Which wolf will win?" The grandfather responds, "The one that gets fed will be the one that wins." The obvious lesson the grandfather is trying to teach is that it makes a difference what we feed our spirit. There are many things you can watch, that you can read, that you can listen to, which might seem harmless, but all of it has an impact upon who we are and how we approach life. There are certain people whose influence makes us better, or worse. Feeding the "good" wolf means consciously and consistently choosing to restrict certain inputs and people from our lives. Choose wisely.

Taking the Easy Road

So, I was talking with a young woman the other day. She is an LPN and working for a home care agency. I asked her about her plans for her future. She responded that she was applying for nursing school. When I asked where, she mentioned a school that was over an hour away. I asked about other schools that were closer and why she chose that particular school. She responded, "I know it is farther away but everyone says it is a lot easier than any of the schools nearby." That is what I am looking for: a nurse who wants the easiest route (NOT). Unfortunately, her perspective is normal; it seems that everyone wants to get the credential, but do the minimum amount of work necessary. It is like the person who asked, "What is the bare minimum I have to do to get to heaven." This mindset has led to a culture of mediocrity. Perhaps it has affected you as well. Are you looking for the easy route? Are you trying to find the path of least resistance? Anything of value that will come into your life will come at the cost of hard work and sacrifice. So, will you settle for mediocrity, or put in the work to find excellence, true satisfaction and joy.

(Your Proverb)

You are a Steward

The Bible says that I (you, too) am created in the image of God. While the actual implications of that are vague, the significance cannot be overlooked. I want to add to being created in the image of God an intersection with this quote: "with great power comes great responsibility." Whether you attribute this saying to Voltaire, who said it first, or Peter Parker, who is most famous for the quote in current times, there is an obvious burden created when taken in light of our creation in the image of God, Maybe a better way to think of it would be, "with human life, comes great responsibility." Stewardship is the awareness of responsibility and the acts necessary to carry out that responsibility. In this case, our Stewardship is over the life that God has given us. Whether in sickness or in health, in good times or bad, for better or worse, our role of Steward over the life God has given us does not diminish or weaken. In fact, and this may seem a paradox to some, the more we embrace that role of Steward, the greater we find our station and satisfaction with our life as a whole. Accept your destiny and fulfill your responsibility.

Worldview?

Every individual has a worldview. Our worldview is influenced by many factors: parental influence, the influence of our friends, the societal values we have been exposed to, faith, and education. The combination of these forces have left us with a worldview through which we interpret everything else that comes to us. Our baseline worldview remains relatively fixed after we reach a certain age, unless it comes into direct contact with contradictory information which cannot be refuted, or which resonates with our deepest psyche. For instance, if your worldview includes bigotry, you have definite, negative, opinions about those who fall into the group toward which you are bigoted. However, when you are faced with other, and compelling, information that your bigotry is unfounded and actually wrong, your worldview will change or you will have to choose to disbelieve the factual evidence. A Christian worldview, as opposed to a secular worldview, means that everything is focused through the lens of what it means to be a person who believes in Jesus Christ as the Son of God and the Bible as the authoritative word of God.

Going Somewhere?

There is a great scene in the movie Sister Act 2, where Sister Mary Clarence is teaching a class and trying to get them to understand the connection between the decisions they make now and the impact it can have on their lives. She does this first be repeating a mantra over and over. Finally, the students turn it into a song. It goes like this: "If you're gonna' be somebody, If you're gonna' go somewhere, you better wake up and pay attention." This is great advice! Just recently, a prominent political figure was being condemned decades after the incident for poor choices made regarding bigotry and discrimination while in college. The decisions we make follow us long after they were made. It is a cautionary tale to wake up and pay attention. This is one reason it is so important to make a connection with Jesus Christ as soon as possible, and then to start living our lives within the boundaries of a Christian worldview which focuses on love and respect for everyone, along with personal integrity and righteousness. The OT prophets said it like this: "For those who have the ears to hear . . . ." I hope that includes you: wake up and pay attention.

Where Does the Bible Fit?

This is a great question and I am glad you asked. The answer has two parts. The first part depends upon your worldview. In another proverb, I have written about worldview and I suggest you check that out. If you do not have a Christian worldview, the Bible, at best, is a book of literature and moral standards. It likely has little or no impact upon your life. If, however, you have a Christian worldview, then the Bible is the foundation for understanding what that worldview means and how a Christian will interact with and view the world. Here is the second part: If you treat the Bible like any other book, that is, read some or all of it and then set it aside, you will be missing the significance of what the Bible really is, and miss the value it can add to your life. The Bible, for a Christian, is not just another book, no matter how good. It is a *living* book. The words between the two covers are more than literature or even law. They communicate the living will of God to a receptive people. The power of the message for the Christian is greater than can be perceived by an unbeliever, but only if refreshed by study and re-reading the truths it holds.

Email Terrorist

An Email Terrorist is someone who uses the carbon copy (cc) feature, or even worse, the blind copy feature (bc) as a weapon. How, you ask? Very simply, when the Email Terrorist receives an email from someone containing information they are at odds with in some way, or even opposed to, they will "reply all" and add other names to the distribution either in the cc or bc fields. Usually the names added are either the other person's supervisor or other persons of influence. Sometimes the reply is an open criticism, other times it is a more subtly worded jab. In either case, by adding individuals to the cc line. The goal is to denigrate the other person's comments at the very least and potentially undercut their credibility. An Email Terrorist is nothing more than a high tech gossip, causing dissention and division. Like a loose cannon rolling around on the ship deck, their comments and the inclusion of others beyond the sphere of the conversation do nothing to help solve the problem, but create mayhem and erode trust. Avoid this practice and deal with each other honestly. Try the Golden Rule.

Execution: Key to Productivity

Execution is a specific set of skills, behaviors, and disciplines that individuals must master in order to accomplish their goals and achieve extraordinary results, in less time, and with better consistency that those who do not have them. These include:

1. Critical thinking that examines all aspects of a problem before drawing conclusions. This includes a discipline that resists making decisions without gathering as much information as is reasonable under the time constraints.
2. Discernment to be able to analyze the data and draw conclusions.
3. The confidence to make a decision based on the analysis and the core values of the person or organization.
4. The strength to resist the nay-sayers and doubters when pursuing a course.
5. The humility to admit responsibility when a decision fails and adjustments have to be made
6. And then be able to do it over and over again.

The course to greatness lies fully in the sphere of execution. Only thought translated into action makes a difference in the long-run.

(Your Proverb)

Conclusion

As you have figured out, these proverbs are only the tip of the iceberg of information that it would have been nice to know before now. I'm sure by now you have already inserted a few of those missing proverbs in the blank pages provided for that purpose. It is my hope that you will continue to refer to this book, perhaps read a proverb three to five days a week and ponder how to apply them in your life, perhaps even share them around the dinner table with your kids.

These are the kinds to things which, in an older time, children would have gleaned from working with their parents around the house, but those days are largely gone. However, the information in these proverbs is still important and will make a difference if applied.

These proverbs are recorded in short YouTube videos under the same name: Proverbs for Living a Fulfilling Life on my YouTube Channel, if you prefer to watch them instead of reading them.

May God richly bless and guide you as you face the challenges of each day.

www.ingramcontent.com/pod-product-compliance
Lightning Source LLC
Chambersburg PA
CBHW031442040426
42444CB00007B/939